Philadelphia with Children

Philadelphia with Children

Elizabeth S. Gephart • Anne S. Cunningham

Illustrated by Candace Stringer

STARRHILL PRESS
Washington & Philadelphia

Published by Starrhill Press
P.O. Box 32342
Washington, DC 20007
(202) 686-6703

Library of Congress Cataloging in Publication Data

Gephart, Elizabeth S., 1957-
Philadelphia with children / Elizabeth S. Gephart, Anne S.
Cunningham ; illustrated by Candace Stringer. — 1st ed.
p. cm.
Includes index.
ISBN 0-913515-34-5
1. Philadelphia (Pa.)—Description—1981- —Guide-books.
2. Family recreation—Pennsylvania—Philadelphia—Guide-books.
I. Cunningham, Anne S., 1946-   . II. Title.
F158.18.G47   1988
917.48'110443—dc19   88-12323
CIP

The authors thank Terry Carstensen, Ann Keech,
Gary Madeira and the many kind curators
who helped with research.

Printed in the United States of America

First edition

1 3 5 7 9 8 6 4 2

To Burgo, Pater, George and Steve, with
many thanks for many years of adventure.
Most of all we dedicate this book
to Anne and Nolie and John and Nan,
for being the reason we wrote it.

CONTENTS

Codes:

♿ Good wheelchair (and stroller) accessibility.

♿ Limited wheelchair accessibility (*see* Appendix B,
page 208, for limitations).

🚌 Programs recommended for school groups.

♀ Membership benefits and discounts available.

✈ Good place for a rainy day outing.

🎂 Birthday party facilities available with advance notice.

Introduction

Like the munchkins in Oz, Philadelphians have been busy cleaning and brushing and polishing their city. Renovation, new construction and pride have made it once again the City of Brotherly Love. It's a great place to explore with children. Independence National Historical Park, home of the Liberty Bell, has more than 50 important sites within a three block area. Museums range from the city's Please Touch Museum for children seven and under to the awesome, medieval castle-like Mercer Museum in Doylestown for older children. Opportunities for fun and active learning are almost endless in the city, in the country, and in nearby New Jersey and Delaware. Lancaster County's Amish country appeals to everyone.

As the title indicates, this book is for adventures *with* children. We encourage adults to participate with youngsters, whether it's for an hour or a full day. The section called "Before You Go" will help with initial planning. More detailed sections in the back of the book list "first-choice" activities, free activities, locations by county, and maps. Another section lists special events according to the month they take place. Of course life with children is not always easy, so there is a Helpful Numbers List with addresses and phone numbers for poison control, hospitals, child abuse helplines, and other emergencies.

Admission times and prices are subject to change without notice. Institutions not set up for children are not listed. We apologize for any omissions or errors and would appreciate hearing from our readers, c/o Starrhill Press, P.O. Box 32342, Washington, DC 20007.

The benefits of an outing with a child are immeasurable. Whether you visit a park down the street or a museum downtown, Philadelphia and the surrounding communities offer countless places to spend that special time together.

E.S.G. and A.S.C.

Handicapped and Special Services

A note from the mother of a disabled child:

Stimulation. All children need it for intellectual, physical and emotional growth. The days of the handicapped child can be filled with therapy, schooling and simply having their needs met. But seeing, feeling and smelling new things stimulates curiosity and can make school and home lessons more significant, away from the pressures to improve.

We have seen our son, Willie, discover and enjoy a whole new world of museums, theater, music, nature and history from his wheelchair. We look for museums with plenty of hands-on activities, theaters with special wheelchair areas (discount tickets may be available), and for easy access on all outings. Repeat visits reinforce and expand the experience. The Please Touch Museum, Schuylkill Valley Nature Center, and the Philadelphia Zoo are extremely accessible and stimulating for our child.

Being out in the world may be your child's future, and now is the time to begin these adventures, with the security of family or friends. Even if his or her future will be a sheltered one, trips to new places and sharing different experiences can awaken new interests and create special memories.

—Willie's Mom

Special Services Phone Numbers: Area code (215)

Accessibility for Independence National Historical Park: 597-7115.

Mayor's Office for the Handicapped: 686-2798 or (TTY) 564-1782 (list of accessible restaurants available).

Carousel House (Dept. of Recreation): 686-0160.

Associated Services for the Blind: 627-0600.

Radio Information Center for the Blind: 627-0600, ext. 205.

Library for the Blind and Physically Handicapped: 925-3213.

Elwy-Nevil Center for Deaf and Hearing Impaired: 895-5509 or (TTY) 895-5695.

Travel Information Service (Moss Rehabilitation Hospital): 456-9900, ext. 9603, or (TTY) 456-9602.

SEPTA and PATCO offer discounts for handicapped riders.

Amtrak Information, for the hearing impaired: (TTY) 1-800-562-6960.

See page 207 for the list of activities with wheelchair access.

Before You Go

Deciding Where To Go

- Independence National Historical Park's Visitor Center (*see* page 15), mid-block on 3rd between Chestnut and Walnut, is the best place to start with a child in search of history. Good movie and lots of information.

- First Choice Activities (*see* page 195) lists some of our own children's favorite activities.

- A Calendar of Special Events (*see* page 197) tells what seasonal events are scheduled each year.

- A Free Activities list (*see* page 205) presents a multitude of things to do without paying an admission fee.
- Weather forecast recording: (215) WE 6-1212.

Eating

- Eating information under each listing indicates picnic areas, in-house snack bars, and restaurants when they're appropriate for younger children.
- If you pack a picnic for a trip to the country, bring a blanket to spread on the ground in case picnic tables are full.
- There is NO FOOD allowed at most nature centers.

Time Needed

- Time allotments under each listing will help even the busiest adult plan time for an adventure with a child. You'd be surprised how much fun you can pack into an hour or two.
- Where there are is no time allotted, you can see the attraction in less than one hour.
- Be sure to add travel time for realistic planning. Nobody likes to be rushed, especially curious youngsters when they're having fun.

Transportation

Air: Philadelphia International Airport is the main airport for the city. To get to Center City, use SEPTA's Airport High Speed Line or drive via Route I-76 or I-95. Alternative airports are Northeast Philadelphia Airport or Wings Field in Blue Bell, PA.

Bus: *See* SEPTA, below.

Car: *See* maps at the back of the book for major routes. Detailed maps of Philadelphia are available at the Visitors Centers at 16th Street and Kennedy Boulevard, and at 3rd and Chestnut Streets. Three Bridges cross the Delaware River from Philadelphia to New Jersey: the Ben Franklin Bridge via Route I-676, the Betsy Ross Bridge off Route I-95, the Walt Whitman Bridge via Route I-76.

- PATCO (Port Authority Transit Corp.) High Speed Line runs between Philadelphia and New Jersey. Leaves from underground stop at 16th and Locust Street, or from underground stops on Market Street at 13th, 10th, and 8th Streets. Information: (215) 922-4600.

- SEPTA (Southeastern PA Transit Authority) covers the major daily routes by bus, trolley, subway and train. Information: (215) 574-7800. Schedules and maps of routes available at SEPTA Information Center, 841 Chestnut Street, Philadelphia, Monday-Friday, 8:30 AM-4:30 PM, or at the SEPTA Customer Service and Sales Office, 15th and Market Streets, underground concourse. "Transpass" gives all-you-can-ride weekly discounts.

- **Subway:** *See* SEPTA and PATCO above.

- **Taxi:** Not always readily available from all locations.

- **Train:** Amtrak into 30th Street Station (30th and Market Streets). Information: (215) 824-1600. ConRail's commuter service is run by SEPTA from all points to three center city rail stations: 30th Street Station (30th and Market), Suburban Station (16th Street and JFK Boulevard), and Market East (Market Street between 10th and 12th Streets). Call SEPTA or your local train station for information.

History

The excitement of being right there, where America was born, is everywhere—in the cities' colonial buildings, across the bumpy battlefields that cover the countryside, and in the elegant mansions preserved from earlier days.

Let the children decide which place they want to visit. Whether they're scrambling around costumed guides in Valley Forge Park or giggling about chamber pots in colonial houses, children find unique angles from which to view our early American heritage. Perhaps the most forgettable was when one of our children asked if we kept mentioning Benjamin Franklin because we knew him when we were young.

Independence National Historical Park is the best place to start with children in Philadelphia . . .

INDEPENDENCE NATIONAL HISTORICAL PARK

Here is an enjoyable, easy history lesson where buildings are within walking distance of each other, the open space behind the buildings along Chestnut and Walnut Streets between 2nd and 5th Streets is lovely and green, and there are plenty of benches where you can rest and talk about what you've seen. Hot dog and snack vendors make it possible to eat on-the-move.

More than 50 historic sites within three square blocks are open to the public on weekends.

There is no admission charge for any Park building; summer hours extend into the evening. Some buildings open only on weekends in winter. For latest recorded information call 627-1776. Park Ranger Guides are in every house and are knowledgeable and pleasant about answering questions.

&. A special Accessibility Guide, available at the Visitor Center, tells where ramps are located. A captioned version of the film, *Independence*, is shown upon request.

We recommend you start with a visit to:

Independence National Historical Park Visitor Center

3rd Street between Chestnut and Walnut Streets
Philadelphia, PA 19106
(215) 597-8974

Hours: Daily 9 AM-5 PM. Closed Christmas and New Year's.

Description: If visitor centers were rated, this would win four stars. It offers free maps that are easy to read, and schedules for more events than you could possibly attend. The staff people we've encountered have been invariably friendly and helpful. A large gift shop sells books and souvenirs. The film, *Independence*, and exhibits like the "Promise of Permanency" send patriotic chills through even the most hardened tourist.

Codes: &. ♅ ⛟

7,000,000 people visit
Independence National
Historical Park each year.

Betsy Ross House

See Glimpses of History, page 26.

Carpenters' Hall

320 Chestnut Street
Philadelphia, PA 19106
(215) 925-0167

Hours: Tuesday-Sunday 10 AM-4 PM; January and February hours shorter, call 627-1776. Closed Thanksgiving, Christmas, New Year's and Easter.

Cost: Free.

Description: Still owned by the Carpenters' Company of Philadelphia, Carpenters' Hall was the meeting place of the First Continental Congress in 1774. Displays show tools and techniques used by early members who were not only skilled craftsmen but also the important architects and builders of early Philadelphia.

Codes: ♿ ✈ 🚌

Congress Hall

6th and Chestnut Streets
Philadelphia, PA 19106
(215) 627-1776 recorded, or 597-4678

Hours: Daily 9 AM-5 PM. Closed Christmas and New Year's.

Cost: Free.

Description: One of the "twin buildings" flanking Independence Hall, this is the one on the west side. Housed the U.S. Congress when Philadelphia was the capital of the United States between 1790-1800. Here George Washington was inaugurated for his second term and John Adams, four years later, was sworn in as President. *See also* Old City Hall, page 20.

Codes: ♿ ✈ 🚌

Edgar Allan Poe National Historic Site

530 North 7th Street
Philadelphia, PA 19123
(215) 597-8780

Hours: Daily 9 AM-5 PM. Closed Christmas and New Year's.

Cost: Free.

Description: Just off the beaten path, this stark house and garden with a large raven statue convey the author's sense of mystery to teen-age and adult fans. Ten-minute slide show and specialized school programs reveal the "Four Faces of Poe." January and October evening candlelight programs celebrate the author's birth and death.

Codes:

Franklin Court

314-322 Market Street
Philadelphia, PA 19106
(215) 597-2760

(Best approach is through an alley off Chestnut between 3rd and 4th Streets, next to the Philadelphia Maritime Museum.)

Hours: Daily 9 AM-5 PM. Closed Christmas and New Year's.

Cost: Free.

Description: Great place to exercise a child's imagination. With no plans of Franklin's house to help them, the Department of the Interior decided to build a mere outline where the house used to be. Combine this structure with domestic artifacts dug from the site and Franklin's lifestyle comes into focus. Adjacent Print Shop and Post Office remind us that he started one of the earliest newspapers and the U.S. Postal Service.

Going down the ramp and into the underground museum feels like Alice's Descent into Franklinland. Glassed-in gallery features many Franklin inventions and push-button comments from famous people. Children love the Franklin Phone Exchange where they can hear how important people, past and present, have viewed Ben Franklin. Continuous animated doll performance of American history-in-the-making appeals to older children; younger ones have trouble with the phrasing taken from original documents of the time. An excellent movie brings the great inventor and his family to life.

Codes:

Graff House

7th and Market Streets
Philadelphia, PA 19106
(215) 627-1776 recorded, or 597-5392

Hours: Daily 9 AM-5 PM; January-February hours shorter, call 627-1776. Closed Christmas and New Year's.

Cost: Free.

Description: Reconstructed boarding house where Thomas Jefferson agonized over the wording of the Declaration of Independence in 1776. Short film about Jefferson.

Codes: ♿ ⛪ 🚐

Independence Hall

Chestnut Street between 5th and 6th Street
Philadelphia, PA 19106
(215) 627-1776 recorded, or 597-7081

Hours: Daily 9 AM-5 PM daily. Closed Christmas and New Year's.

Cost: Free.

Description: Originally the State House for the Colony of Pennsylvania, this is where the Second Continental Congress met in 1775 and ultimately signed the Declaration of Independence on July 4, 1776. In 1787, the United States Constitution was signed in this room.

The hushed majesty of the antique furniture, green baize-covered tables, and silver ink stands with quills leave no doubt in the visitor's mind of the importance of Independence Hall. Guided tours are free but mandatory, starting in the East Wing. (Don't worry, signs point the way.)

Codes: ♿ ⛪ 🚐

Delaware was the first state to ratify the Constitution, Pennsylvania was the second, and New Jersey the third.

Kosciuszko National Memorial

3rd and Pine Streets
Philadelphia, PA 19106
(215) 627-1776 recorded, or 597-9618

Hours: 9 AM-5 PM daily; January-February hours shorter, call 627-1776. Closed Christmas and New Year's.

Cost: Free.

Description: English and Polish language push-button tapes describe the famous Polish engineer who lived in Philadelphia in 1797 and 1798. Short 7-minute slide show reviews his design of West Point and other interesting accomplishments. Group portrait in the lobby pays tribute to the many foreigners, such as Lafayette and Kosciuszko, who affected the course of the American Revolution.

Codes: ♿ 🛗 🚐

Liberty Bell Pavilion

Independence Mall, Market Street between 5th and
  6th Streets
Philadelphia, PA 19106
(215) 627-1776 recorded, or 597-7624

Hours: Daily 9 AM-5 PM. Closed Christmas and New Year's.

Cost: Free.

Description: The Park Service maintains a supply of enthusiastic guides who tell the story of the Liberty Bell almost nonstop and seem pleased to answer questions from visitors. A great place to start your tour—the excitement over the significance of this single object is contagious. Liberty is, after all, what the Revolution was all about.

Codes: ♿ 🛗 🚐

New Hall

(Marine Corps Memorial Museum)
Chestnut Street between 3rd and 4th Streets
Philadelphia, PA 19106
(215) 627-1776 recorded

Hours: Daily 9 AM-5 PM; January-February hours are shorter, call 627-1776. Closed Christmas and New Year's.

Cost: Free.

Description: Exhibits show Marine Corps' role in American Revolution. Combine with visit to Pemberton House.

Codes: ♿ 🛗 🚐

Old City Hall

5th and Chestnut Streets
Philadelphia, PA 19106
(215) 627-1776 recorded

Hours: Daily 9 AM-5 PM. Closed Christmas and New Year's.

Cost: Free.

Description: One of the "twin buildings" flanking Independence Hall. This is the one on the east side. Original City Hall for Philadelphia, home of U.S. Supreme Court, 1791-1800. Exhibits change periodically. *See also* Congress Hall, page 16.

Codes: ♿ ✤ 🚐

Pemberton House

(Army Navy Museum)
Chestnut Street between 3rd and 4th Streets
Philadelphia, PA 19106
(215) 627-1776 recorded, or 597-2458

Hours: Daily 9 AM-5 PM; January-February hours are shorter, call 627-1776. Closed Christmas and New Year's.

Cost: Free.

Description: Collection of Army and Navy war souvenirs ranges from cannons and guns to flags and uniforms. One room is constructed like the deck of an old war ship, with the feeling of adventure right around the corner. Life size figures and a 12-minute movie about the Revolution are just right for holding a child's attention.

Codes: ♿ ✤ 🚐

Pennsylvania Horticultural Society

See Gardens and Arboretums, page 93.

Second Bank of the United States

420 Chestnut Street
Philadelphia, PA 19106
(215) 627-1776 recorded, or 597-9579

Hours: Daily, 9 AM-5 PM. Closed Christmas and New Year's.

Cost: Free.

Description: Architect William Strickland designed this model of the Parthenon but limited the colonnades to each end. Portrait Gallery inside features prominent figures in American History from 1774-1800.

Codes: ✤ 🚐

FAIRMOUNT PARK

Philadelphia, PA 19131
(215) 686-0001

Fairmount Park, with nearly 9,000 acres, is the largest landscaped city park in the world. Its magnificent waterways and greenscapes, historic buildings and public facilities have graced Philadelphia for the past two hundred years. Site of America's Centennial birthday celebration, Fairmount Park in the 1880s was beautifully landscaped and alive with activity.

Many of the historic mansions standing today in the East and West Park were originally country houses for wealthy families who lived downtown (see Park Houses, below). The Schuylkill River, immortalized by Thomas Eakins's oarsmen, still teems with rowing clubs. The buildings of Boathouse Row outlined with lights after dark provide a visual treat for children traveling along the Schuylkill Expressway or the West River Drive. Joggers, walkers, bikers and picnic lovers dot the river banks almost all year 'round.

The Park provides numerous facilities where athletes congregate for formal and informal games of baseball, soccer, and tennis. Swimming in the summer and sledding in the winter appeal to everyone. About 100 miles of bridle paths weave through the fields and woods for the enjoyment of both horseback riders and walkers (see Park Chart, page 141).

Tributary creeks and their individual parks constitute nearly three-quarters of the total Fairmount Park system. Cobbs Creek Park (780 acres), Pennypack Park (1600 acres), Tacony Creek Park (250 acres), and Wissahickon Park (1700 acres) are part of a massive watershed and land preservation system, with open land, woods, footpaths and few facilities beyond the brilliance provided by Mother Nature. Small bikepath maps for each area are available through the Fairmount Park office (call 686-0001). To get a true feeling for the unique history swirling around each creek, look for detailed maps of these parks in local bookstores.

The best way to get an overview of the Park with children is to take a Fairmount Park Trolley/Bus Tour. Since schedules change according to the season, call 879-4044 for information. See also Fairmount Park map, page 228.

The following Fairmount Park attractions are most likely to appeal to children:

Andorra Natural Area

Old Northwestern Avenue, Chestnut Hill
Philadelphia, PA 19118
(215) 242-5610

Hours: Outdoor natural area is always open. Call for Tree House hours.

Cost: Free.

Description: Rustic nature center welcomes children and lets them touch everything from antlers and porcupine quills to a turtle, snake or rabbit. Discovery Table for toddlers. Beautiful outdoor walking and bridle trails.

Time Needed: ½ hour inside.

Codes: 🚐 🎷 at Tree House/Visitor's Center.

Bartram's House and Gardens

See Gardens and Arboretums, page 89.

Fairmount Water Works

On Schuylkill River beside Philadelphia Museum of Art
Philadelphia, PA 19101
(215) 686-0001, ask for Water Works Restoration Office

Description: Originally a steam pumping station, then an aquarium, and once more under restoration. Children's favorite view of the Water Works is from across the river (on the Schuylkill Expressway) after dark when fully outlined with lights as a continuation of Boat House Row.

Horticulture Center

North Horticultural Drive off Belmont Avenue
Philadelphia, PA 19131
(215) 686-0096

Hours: Monday-Sunday 9 AM-3 PM.

Cost: $1.00 donation.

Description: Horticulture Center stands on the grounds of the Centennial's Horticulture Hall, demolished in the 1950s. The arboretum and flower-filled greenhouses are great for lifting the spirits any time of year. The annual September Harvest Show has many children's activities: competitions for the best vegetable grown over the summer, for creatures made of seeds and pods, for pumpkin painting, and more. Don't miss this low-key, uncrowded, home gardener's autumn version of the more famous Philadelphia Flower Show.

Codes: ♿ 🎷

Japanese House

Near Horticulture Center
North Horticultural Drive off Belmont Avenue
Philadelphia, PA 19131
(215) 686-0096

Hours: May through October, Wednesday-Sunday 10 AM-4 PM. Closed October-early May.

Cost: $1.00 per person.

Description: Beautiful Japanese architecture, furniture and landscape combine to create a tranquil refuge from city life. Call for schedule of tea ceremonies and other demonstrations.

Codes: 🕮 🚌

Laurel Hill Cemetery

3822 Ridge Avenue
Philadelphia, PA 19123
(215) 228-8200

Description: As daring, adventuresome outings go, this has tremendous appeal. Giant mausoleums and monuments, sculptures and tombstones light the imaginations of children of all ages. The grave of Sarah Josepha Hale, who wrote "Mary Had a Little Lamb," is here. Authority John Francis Marion tells about veterans of all wars, from the Revolution to Vietnam, who are buried here. Marion runs a thrilling tour of the cemetery for several evenings around Halloween (*see* Calendar of Events, October).

Memorial Hall

North Concourse Drive and Parkside Avenue
Philadelphia PA 19131
(215) 686-0001

Description: Originally built for the Centennial celebration, this awesome building contains a replica of the Centennial Fairgrounds. The Park Commission Office is housed here and offers Fairmount Park information.

Pennypack Environmental Center

See Nature, page 103.

Philadelphia Zoo

See Zoos, page 109.

Rittenhousetown

Lincoln Drive at Wissahickon Avenue
Philadelphia, PA 19144
(215) 843-0943

Hours: #207 Lincoln Drive (only house open to public): April-October, Saturday and Sunday 12 Noon-4 PM. Rittenhousetown Open House weekend in September.

Cost: Free.

Description: America's first paper mill was built here in 1690. Visitors with good imaginations enjoy strolling around the grounds, though most of the buildings are private property, open only during the September festival weekend.

Smith Civil War Monument

Centennial and Lansdowne Drives across from Memorial Hall
Philadelphia, PA 19131

Description: Tall granite towers are known to children as the "whispering benches". Try sitting at one corner of the curved stone bench and whispering a message to a friend sitting at the other corner of the bench.

Smith Memorial Playgrounds and Playhouse

Reservoir Drive near 33rd Street
Philadelphia, PA 19121
(215) PO 5-4325

Hours: Monday-Saturday 9 AM-5 PM (to 4:30 in winter). Swimming pool for young children opens mid-June.

Cost: Free.

Description: It seems incredible that Mr. and Mrs. Richard Smith built this huge house and playground in 1899 just for Philadelphia's children. Giant platform sliding board, swings, and dozens of structures to climb outside. The basement of this mansion-just-for-children features cars for the very young, painted streets, stop lights, and a gas station. Other floors offer a multitude of activities for children under the age of 12.

Driving: Kelly Drive to Grant's Statue. Turn onto Fountain Green Drive. Take the first right then bear right at the Yield sign. Follow signs.

Codes: ♿ ✈ 🚐 ⛵

Park Houses

There are plenty of antiques with curious appeal for children among the fine collections: tea caddies with locks on them because tea was so valuable; long white pipes in a dining room, for passing around after a meal—as each person took a puff, the tip was cut off before it was handed to the next. Chamounix is the first city-owned youth hostel in the country and has hosted young people from all over the world. Strawberry Mansion's third floor (attic) has doll houses and children's toys. Mount Pleasant has a child's crib attached to a canopy bed so parent and child were always together. Mount Pleasant was supposed to be the home for newly married Benedict Arnold and his wife, but he was convicted of treason before he could move in.

Woodford has our favorite collection of toys, games, knick-knacks and several handcarved Schimmel animals. The pewter "Inner and Outer Man" in the kitchen served as hand or foot or beverage warmer outside in a carriage, then came inside to be a bed warmer. Holiday House Tours in December appeal to all ages. Visit the houses by car or by Fairmount Park Trolley. Call (215) 879-4044 for trolley schedules.

Belmont Mansion
West Fairmount Park
(215) 878-8844

Cedar Grove
Lansdowne Drive, off
N. Concourse Drive
East Fairmount Park
(215) 763-8100, ext. 332

Chamounix Youth Hostel
North end of
West Fairmount Park
(215) 878-3676

Laurel Hill
East Edgely Drive
East Fairmount Park
(215) 235-1776

Lemon Hill
Kelly and Sedgeley Drives
East Fairmount Park
(215) 232-4337

Mount Pleasant
Mount Pleasant Drive
West Fairmount Park
(215) 763-8100, ext. 333

Ormiston
Ormiston Drive
East Fairmount Park
(215) 763-2222 (answers
Royal Heritage Society)

Strawberry Mansion
33rd and Dauphin Streets
East Fairmount Park
(215) 228-8364

Sweetbrier Mansion
Fairmount Park West
(215) 222-1333

Woodford
33rd and Dauphin Streets
East Fairmount Park
(215) 229-6115

GLIMPSES OF HISTORY

Barns-Brinton House

P.O. Box 27, Route 1
Chadds Ford, PA 19317
(215) 388-7376

Hours: June, July and August, Saturday-Sunday 10 AM-
5 PM. Groups welcome anytime by appointment.

Cost: $1.00 adults, $.50 children.

Description: Guides in colonial costume explain life as it
once was in this 18th-century tavern. Colonial craft
demonstrations.

Driving: I-95 south, Rte..322 west, then left on Rte. 1. House
is 1½ miles south of Chadds Ford.

Codes: 🦌 🚐 ⚘

Bartram's House and Gardens

See Gardens and Arboretums, page 89.

Betsy Ross House

239 Arch Street
Philadelphia, PA 19107
(215) 627-5343

Hours: Daily 9 AM-5 PM. Closed major holidays.

Cost: Free.

Description: Seamstress Ross's colonial house is restored
and set with manikins and period furniture to give a good
idea of what life was like when George Washington ordered the
first American flag. Glassed-in-rooms keep visitors in a one-
way traffic flow along the narrow staircase. Courtyard is a nice
place for weary young tourists to rest.

Codes: 🦌 🚐

The state bird of
Pennsylvania is
the ruffed grouse.

Brandywine Battlefield State Park

P.O. Box 202, Route 1
Chadds Ford, PA 19317
(215) 459-3342

Hours:
Visitor Center: Tuesday-Saturday 9 AM-5 PM (houses close at
4 PM), Sunday 12 Noon-5 PM (houses close at 4 PM).
Battlefield Park grounds: September-May, Tuesday-Saturday
9 AM-5 PM; Memorial Day-Labor Day, Tuesday-Saturday
9 AM-8 PM, Sunday 12 Noon-8 PM

Cost: $1.00 adults (slide show, exhibits and houses), $.50
children 6-18, under 6 free.

Description: Permanent and rotating exhibits offer a lively
education about the American Revolution. Washington's and
Lafayette's headquarters have been reconstructed to evoke the
atmosphere of the ill-fated Battle of Brandywine.

Time Needed: Minimum 1 hour.

Tours/Programs: House tours and variety of programs
throughout the year. May and September battle re-enactments
in full costume delight youngsters.

Eating: Picnic tables at regular intervals in the park.

Driving: I-95 south, Rte. 322 W, then left on Rte. 1 south.
Watch for signs on your right in the Chadds Ford area.

Codes: ♿ 🚌

Brinton 1704 House

Oakland Road
West Chester, PA 19380
(215) 793-1072, or 692-4800

Hours: May-October, Tuesday, Thursday, Saturday 1-4 PM.
Closed holidays. Groups by appointment.

Cost: Donation requested.

Description: Authentic restoration based on the 1751 house
inventories. Fancy leaded windows, indoor bake oven, raised
hearth, and colonial herb garden appeal to children.

Driving: I-95 south, Rte. 322 west, Rte. 1 south, Rte. 100
north. At Dilworthtown, turn left onto Oakland Road and
watch for house on your left.

Codes: 🚶 🚌

Bucks County Covered Bridges

c/o Bucks County Tourist Commission
152 Swamp Road
Doylestown, PA 18901
(215) 345-4552

Description: There are many stories about the existence of covered bridges, from the romantic to the practical notion of protecting animals from their natural fear of crossing over water. The Bucks County Tourist Commission offers a map by mail to guide you on a circular tour of its thirteen covered bridges.

Burlington County Historical Loops

The Burlington County Cultural and Heritage Commission
49 Rancocas Road, Mount Holly, NJ 08060
(609) 265-5068

A four-page pamphlet brings to life 28 historical buildings and Revolutionary War sites in western New Jersey. Drive your own car along the Northern Loop from Bordentown to Mount Holly or the Southern Loop from Mount Holly to Batsto.

Chad House

P.O. Box 27, Route 100
Chadds Ford, PA 19317
(215) 388-1132, or 388-7376

Hours: June, July and August, Saturday-Sunday 10 AM-5 PM. Group tours available year around by appointment.

Cost: $1.00 adults, $.50 children.

Description: Stone building was the home of John Chad, for whom Chadds Ford was named. Guides in colonial costume describe life in 18th-century Brandywine Valley. See how they baked in a beehive oven.

Driving: I-95 south, Rte. 322 west, Rte. 1 south. At Chadds Ford, go right onto Rte. 100 north. House is ¼ mile ahead.

Codes: ⚓ 🚌 ♿

Delancey Street

Between Spruce and Pine, and 2nd and 4th Streets
Philadelphia, PA 19106

Description: A short walk down these two blocks gives a great impression of cobblestone streets and the historic houses of Old Philadelphia. *See also* Elfreth's Alley and Head House Square.

Elfreth's Alley

2nd Street between Arch and Race Streets
Philadelphia, PA 19106
(215) 574-0560

Description: Oldest continuously occupied street in America. Cobblestones and "busybodies" (mirrors by the second floor windows for checking your neighbor's activities) are just a few of the quaint features. #126 is the Elfreth's Alley Museum, open 10 AM-4 PM daily. The other houses are occupied, but they are open to the public once a year, on the first Sunday in June from 12 Noon-5 PM.

Franklin's Bust

4th and Arch Streets
Philadelphia, PA 19106

Description: Philadelphia school children donated 80,000 pennies to create this large, amiable outdoor bust of Ben Franklin.

George Read II House and Garden

42 The Strand
New Castle, DE 19720
(302) 322-8411

Hours: January-February, Saturday 10 AM-4 PM, Sunday 12 Noon-4 PM; March 1-December 31, Tuesday-Saturday 10 AM-4 PM, Sunday 12 Noon-4 PM.

Cost: $3.00 adults, $1.50 children through age 18.

Description: Early 19th-century owner's style contrasts with 20th-century owner's taste, preserved in three rooms. Beautiful grounds, museum shop and tour of New Castle complete the picture for children.

Driving: I-95 south past Wilmington. Take Rte. 141 south towards New Castle for approximately 4 miles and turn left onto Rte. 9. Go over an overpass, straight at Yield sign (road turns into Delaware Avenue). Turn left onto 2nd Street, right onto Harmony, right onto The Strand (best to park on Delaware Avenue and walk from there).

Codes: 🚐 �

Germantown

See Unique Areas, page 162.

Graeme Park

859 County Line Road
Horsham, PA 19044
(215) 343-0965

Hours: Wednesday-Saturday 9 AM-5 PM, Sunday 12 Noon-5 PM. OPEN on Memorial Day, July 4th and Labor Day.

Cost: $1.50 adults, $.50 children 6-17, under 6 free.

Description: Beautiful setting with ducks and sheep. 40-minute house tour emphasizes architectural form and function such as that of the open-hearth kitchen.

Tours/Programs: Special children's tour with advance notice.

Driving: PA Turnpike to Willow Grove Exit, to Rte. 611 north. Left at County Line Road, then watch for sign on your left.

Codes: 🐎 🚐

The Grange

Myrtle Avenue at Warwick Road
Havertown, PA 19083
(215) 446-4958

Hours: April-December, Saturday-Sunday 1-4 PM.

Cost: $1.50 adults, $.75 children.

Description: Mansion house, formal gardens, springhouse, carriage house, summer kitchen, root cellar and outhouse give visitors a good idea of how estates were run in the 18th and 19th centuries. Inside, children love the second-floor bureau with hidden drawers and locks. Outside, the woodland path, foot bridges and water wheel appeal to all ages.

Driving: I-76 (Schuylkill Expressway) to City Avenue exit. Go west on City Avenue for 4½ miles, go right at Earlington Road, then right on Bennington. Go just the length of two houses, watch for Grange signs and turn left on Myrtle. House is two blocks ahead, right turn through gate beyond church.

Codes: 🐎 🚐

Green Hills Farm
(The Pearl S. Buck Home)

Perkasie, PA 18944
(215) 249-0100, or 242-6779
(800) 242-BUCK (from outside the Philadelphia area)

Hours: April-December, tours Monday-Friday 10:30 AM and 2 PM; May-September, tours Sunday 1:30 and 2 PM. Closed mid-January through February, holidays and holiday weekends.

Cost: $4.00 adults, $3.00 children, $10.00 family.

Description: Novelist Pearl Buck devoted herself to helping Amerasian children living in the Orient. The Foundation continues this tradition while honoring her memory and her work, much of which was written right here. House museum and surrounding land provide a nice outing.

Driving: PA Turnpike to Willow Grove Exit, then Rte. 611 north into Doylestown. Go left onto Rte. 313 west into Dublin and left onto Maple Avenue. Green Hills Farm is 1 mile ahead on the right.

Codes: ♿ 🍴 🚐 🐾

Grundy Museum

610 Radcliffe Street
Bristol, PA 19007
(215) 788-9432

Hours: Monday-Friday 1-4 PM.

Cost: Free.

Description: Victorian home of Joseph R. Grundy with all its original furnishings.

Driving: PA Turnpike east to Delaware Valley Interchange. Continue straight across the interchange to get onto Rte. 13 north. At the light go right onto Green Lane, follow to the end, then go right onto Radcliffe Street. Museum is on left.

Codes: 🍴 🚐

Hagley Museum and Eleutherian Mills

Route 100 at Route 141
Greenville, Wilmington, DE 19807
(302) 658-2401

Hours: January 2-March 31, Monday-Friday 1-4:30 PM, weekends 9:30-4:30; April-December, daily 9:30 AM-4:30 PM.

Cost: $6.00 adults, $5.00 students and senior citizens, $2.50 children 6-14, under 6 free.

Description: Restored powder works are just the beginning of this 19th-century industrial community. From the magnificent duPont family residence and garden to the working water wheel to the restored millworker's house and school for mill children, there is a lot to see. Flour mill in operation, 19th-century machine shop, tools and weather vane collections, Sunday school setting and more. Recommended for children ages 5 and up.

Time Needed: ½ day to 1 day.

Tours/Programs: Tours and programs can be as detailed as your child's (or group's) mind can handle.

Eating: Picnic area, refreshments.

Driving: I-95 south to exit 7. Take Rte. 52 north for approximately 3 miles to Rte. 141 north. Follow Rte. 141 north for 100 yards, take first left (not marked), and follow signs for Museum on left.

Codes: 🦽 🚐 ♫

Head House Square and New Market

2nd Street and Pine Street
Philadelphia, PA 19147

Description: Reconstructed colonial marketplace. Programs and fairs throughout the summer months.

Hans Herr House

See Lancaster, page 175.

Delaware's nicknames are the Diamond State, the First State, and the Blue Hen State.

Historic Yellow Springs

P.O. Box 627, Art School Road
Chester Springs, PA 19425
(215) 827-7414

Hours: Monday-Friday 9 AM-4 PM, weekends by reservation. Closed holidays.

Cost: Donation requested.

Description: 140 acres with mineral springs, springhouse and small village. Best to visit during special events like "Sundaes on Sundays" in June, July, and August. Call for dates.

Driving: PA Turnpike to King of Prussia exit, take Rte. 202 south toward West Chester. Exit onto Rte. 401, go right for 5 or 6 miles, take another right onto Rte. 113. Continue for several miles. Watch for signs for Historic Yellow Springs.

Codes: ♀

Hope Lodge and Mather Mill

553 Bethlehem Pike
Fort Washington, PA 19034
(215) 646-1595

Hours: Tuesday-Saturday 9 AM-12 Noon and 1-5 PM, Sunday 12 Noon-5 PM. OPEN Memorial Day, July 4 and Labor Day.

Cost: $1.50 adults, $1.00 children and senior citizens.

Description: Georgian mansion, gardens and grounds. Compare the lifestyles and furnishings of the original 18th-century owners with those of its 20th-century inhabitants who thought they were imitating colonial styles. Excellent children's programs let them handle reproductions of lighting devices, cooking utensils and clothing. Young children learn and sing colonial songs while they watch a fireplace cooking demonstration.

Driving: PA Turnpike to Fort Washington Exit. Go straight on Pennsylvania Avenue (not marked), stay in left lane. At third light, go left onto Bethlehem Pike. Hope Lodge is ¾ mile ahead on left.

Codes: ♠ ⸸ 🚐 ♀

Massey House

P.O. Box 18
Lawrence and Springhouse Roads
Broomall, PA 19008
(215) 353-3644

Hours: April-November, Sunday 2-4:30 PM; June, July, August, Monday-Friday 10 AM-4 PM.

Cost: $1.50 adults, $1.00 children.

Description: Tour includes house and gardens of the early English Quaker settler, Thomas Massey. Junior Guide program for children over age 11 lets them dip candles and make authentic colonial costumes while they learn all about the house and its furnishings. Then Junior Guides participate in programs throughout the year.

Tours/Programs: School programs Spring and Fall by reservation.

Driving: From Philadelphia, take Market St. west onto Rte. 3 (West Chester Pike). Cross Rte. 1 (City Ave.) and go left onto Lawrence Road. Springhouse comes in on the right; house is on corner.

Codes: ⚓ 🚐 ♞

Morton Homestead

Route 420, 100 Lincoln Avenue
Prospect Park, PA 19076
(215) 583-7221

Hours: Wednesday-Saturday 10 AM-4 PM, Sunday 12 Noon-4 PM. Closed January and February.

Cost: $1.00 adults, $.50 children.

Description: Earliest documented log cabin in the United States, dating back to 1650s. Built by the *great-grandfather* of John Morton who signed the Declaration of Independence.

Time Needed: 30-minute tour.

Eating: Picnic area in Governor Printz Park.

Driving: I-95 south from Philadelphia, turn north on Rte. 420. Log House is on your left about 100 yards ahead, but continue past house and look for left-turn signs.

Codes: 🚐

Old Dutch House

32 East Third Street
New Castle, DE 19720
(302) 322-9168

Hours: April-November, Tuesday-Saturday 11 AM-4 PM.

Cost: $1.00 per person.

Description: Reputed to be the oldest brick dwelling in Delaware. Tin glazed earthenware and other collections from the Dutch Colonial period.

Driving: I-95 south, Rte. 41 south into New Castle, then left onto Rte. 9 which runs into Delaware Avenue. Park on Delaware Avenue. House on 3rd Street near Courthouse.

Codes: 🐎 🚐

Old Fort Mifflin

Fort Mifflin Road, near Phila. International Airport
Philadelphia, PA 19153
(215) 365-9781

Hours: March-December, weekends 12 Noon-4:30 PM.

Cost: $.50 adults, $.25 children.

Description: Built during the Revolutionary War and used again during the Civil War as soldiers' quarters. The bunkers were used to store supplies and prisoners. The Fort was again used for weapons and ammunition storage during World War II and the Korean War. Although the guides bring the Fort to life with historical anecdotes, its current condition does discourage some visitors.

Eating: Picnic area.

Driving: I-95 south to Enterprise Ave. Exit. Follow Enterprise Ave. to where it veers to the right. Go to the left onto Old Fort Mifflin Road. Fort on right. Watch for signs.

Codes: ♿

Old Town Hall

512 Market Street Mall
Wilmington, DE 19801
(302) 655-7161

Hours: March-December, Tuesday-Friday 12 Noon-4 PM,
Saturday 10 AM-4 PM. Closed major holidays and during exhibition changes.

Cost: Free.

Description: Changing displays of Delaware regional art,
children's toys and items of local interest. Restored jail cells in
the basement may appeal to children more than the political
significance of the chambers above.

Driving: I-95 south to Wilmington Boulevard Exit. Turn onto
Wilmington Boulevard, stay in left lane and follow signs to
Orange Street. Take left onto Orange, right on 6th St. and
park. (Market Street is a mall—no vehicles allowed.)

Codes: ♿ ✝ 🚐 ⚘

Penn's Landing:
USS *Becuna,* USS *Olympia,*
Moshulu and *Gazela of Philadelphia*

Delaware River waterfront, between Market and Lombard
Philadelphia, PA 19106
(215) 922-1898

Hours: USS *Olympia* and USS *Becuna:* summer, daily
10 AM-5 PM; winter, daily 10 AM-4:30 PM. Closed Christmas
and New Year's.

Cost: $3.00 adults, $1.50 children under 12 (for both ships).

Description: *Becuna* gives new meaning to the idea of
crowded quarters and life on a submarine. *Olympia* is famous
for Commodore George Dewey and "Fire when ready, Gridley"
at Manila Bay. *Moshulu,* the largest steel sailing ship in the
world, is now a restaurant, but there is a small museum
upstairs. *Gazela* is a 102-year-old, three-masted tall ship at
Dock Street; go through her when she's in port. *See* Workshop
on the Water, page 70.

Time Needed: 1-2 hours.

Eating: Continue the maritime theme by eating on the
Moshulu, or buy from any Penn's Landing vendors.

Codes: 🚐

Pennsbury Manor

Route 9
Morrisville, PA 19067
(215) 946-0400

Hours: March-December, Tuesday-Saturday 9 AM-5 PM,
Sunday 12 Noon-5 PM.

Cost: $2.50 adults, $1.75 senior citizens, $1.00 children,
under 6 free.

Description: William Penn would be thrilled to see all the
activity at his country estate. Enjoy the kitchen garden, the formal garden, the livestock (sheep, a donkey, a peacock), and the
beautiful Delaware River view. To better understand 17th-
century life, try the brief slide show inside or take the 1½ hour
tour from busy woodworker's shop to smoke house to elegant
manor house. First Sunday in each month from April to
November are Living History Sundays. Colonial craft series all
year. Children's items in gift shop.

Time Needed: ½ day.

Tours/Programs: "Mondays at the Manor" are workshops for
4- and 5-year-olds with an adult. Summer camps emphasize
history, crafts, and colonial way of life. Good opportunities for
teen-age volunteers all summer.

Eating: Picnic pavilion.

Driving: PA Turnpike to Exit 29 (Bristol). Follow Rte. 13
north for 2½ miles. After RR station, take sharp right onto
overpass (no street sign). At dead end, turn left onto Main St.
Follow Main St. (road changes names) for 2½ miles to Pennsbury Rd. Follow signs for Pennsbury Manor.

Codes: ♿ 🚐 ♟

Pennsylvania is the 33rd largest state,
and covers 44,888 square miles.

Pennypacker Mills

Route 73 and Haldeman Road
Schwenksville, PA 19473
(215) 287-9349

Hours: Tuesday-Saturday 10 AM-4 PM, Sunday 1-4 PM.
Closed Mondays and holidays.

Cost: Free.

Description: Visitors get a feeling for the Pennypacker family
that lived here almost 100 years ago. Children are welcome to
touch the arrowheads and other Indian and Revolutionary
War treasures collected on the property.

Driving: I-76 (Schuylkill Expressway) west, Rte. 202 south,
Rte. 422 west to Collegeville. Take Rte. 29 north for about
8 miles. Look for signs for Rte. 73, and turn right onto it.
Pennypacker Mills is on the left immediately after you cross
the bridge.

Codes: 🚶 🚌

Port of History Museum

See Museums, page 72.

Rickett's Circus

12th and Market Streets
Philadelphia, PA 19107

Description: Tiny circular brick park. America's first circus
building opened here in 1793. In April that year, British equestrian John Bill Rickett gave the first complete circus performance in America. Later in the season, President Washington
attended this show.

Rock Ford Plantation

See Lancaster page 179.

Rockwood

610 Shipley Road
Wilmington, DE 19809
(302) 571-7776

Hours: Tuesday-Saturday 11 AM-4 PM.

Cost: $3.00 adults, $2.50 senior citizens, $1.00 children 5-16. Free self-guided tours of grounds only.

Description: Rural Gothic 19th-century manor. Estate includes manor house, conservatory, carriage house, and beautiful landscaped gardens. Guided tours include small boy's room and explanations of how children lived in 1892. *See* Gothic Gables and Fables in Calendar of Events, October.

Driving: I-95 south to exit 9 (Marsh Road). Turn left onto Marsh Rd., right onto Washington St. extension. At first light, turn right onto Shipley Rd. Rockwood is on left.

Codes: ♿ 🚌 👁

Smithville Mansion

See Villages and Homesteads, page 50.

Delaware's northern boundary is a perfect arc with a 12-mile radius. The center of the circle was originally the cupola of the old Dover courthouse.

Valley Forge National Historic Park

Valley Forge, PA 19481-0953
(215) 783-1077

Hours: Daily, dawn to dusk. Visitors Center and Museum, daily 9 AM-4:30 PM.

Cost: Free, but some buildings have small charge.

Description: Not a soldiers' battlefield, but a field of battle between man and nature. Short movie in Visitor's Center conveys the winter hardships of the Continental Army in 1778. After film, ask for the free Children's Discovery Guide pamphlet and explore the park by foot, bike, car or bus. Information cassettes available for rent, mid-April to October. Guides dressed in costume add realism, fun and stories when visitors stop at the log cabins. Local residents come on Sundays to watch radio controlled model airplanes fly at the Park entrance near Rte. 202.

Time Needed: 1 hour to 1 day.

Tours/Programs: Ranger's Choice Program on Saturday mornings: join a Park Ranger for his favorite walk and talk. Ask to see site of archaeological digs—kids are thrilled as workers dig up musket balls, dish fragments, etc.

Eating: Picnic at Varnum's, Wayne's Woods, and Betzwood.

Driving: I-76 (Schuylkill Expressway) to Exit 25. Follow North Gulph Rd. for 2½ miles to Visitor's Center on left.

Codes: ♿ 🍴 🚐 (Visitor's Center and film)

Walt Whitman Home State Historic Site

330 Mickle Boulevard
Camden, NJ
(609) 964-5383

Hours: Wednesday-Friday 9 AM-12 Noon and 1-6 PM, Saturday 10 AM-12 Noon and 1-6 PM, Sunday 1-6 PM.

Cost: Free.

Description: Whitman's home from 1884 until his death in 1892. Guide tells anecdotes about the poet; children love the personal artifacts, even his hair.

Driving: Cross to N.J. on Ben Franklin Bridge, then right on Broadway to 5th light. Go right on Mickle Boulevard to #330.

Codes: 🍴 🚐 ♿

Washington Crossing Historic Park

Washington Crossing, PA 18977
(215) 493-4076

Hours: Grounds: daily 9:00 AM-8 PM.
Buildings: Monday-Saturday 9 AM-5 PM, Sunday 12 Noon-5 PM.

Cost: Free, but some buildings have admission charge.

Description: Film of Washington crossing the Delaware shown every 1½ hours in the Visitor's Center. Tours of the houses leave after each film showing. Bowman's Hill Tower, with 121 steps, uses up lots of kid-energy. Otherwise, just wander across this beautiful countryside or follow wildflower paths at Bowman's Hill Wildflower Preserve.

Time Needed: Minimum 2 hours.

Eating: Picnic pavilions on the property.

Driving: I-95 north to New Hope/Yardley exit, go left onto Taylorsville Road for 3 miles. Then right on Rte. 532, left on Rte. 32 (River Road). Parking on left, Visitor's Center on right.

Codes: ♿ 🚻 🚐

Weavertown One-Room Schoolhouse

See Lancaster, page 181.

Wheatland

See Lancaster, page 181.

The first governor of Pennsylvania, from 1785 to 1788, was Ben Franklin.

Winterthur

Route 5
Winterthur, DE 19735
(302) 654-1548

Hours: Tuesday-Saturday 10 AM-4 PM, Sunday 12 Noon-4 PM. Closed major holidays.

Cost: Varies for different activities.

Description: Perfection everywhere. Children enjoy the 45-minute Garden Tram Tour in Spring, and the Two Centuries Tour of the famous museum collection. Children not allowed on some tours. Visitor's Center gift shop has whole room devoted to children's toys, books and treasures.

Time Needed: 2 hours or more.

Tours/Programs: Museum by tour only. Call or write for brochures of the many educational tours available.

Eating: Family-style restaurant in Visitor's Center.

Driving: I-95 south to Exit 7 (Delaware Avenue). Follow Rte. 52 north six miles to Winterthur. OR: Rte. 1 south, left on Rte. 52, Winterthur on your left.

Codes: ♿ 🦌 🚐 ♀

Delaware is the second smallest state.
It is 96 miles long, 35 miles wide and
covers 1,978 square miles.

HISTORICAL SOCIETIES AND MUSEUMS

Some of the greatest treasures are kept right in our own back yard.

Historical Society of Delaware: (302) 322-8411
(George Read II House)

New Jersey State Historic Commission: (609) 292-6062
Burlington County Historical Society: (609) 386-4773
Camden County Historical Society: (609) 964-3333
Gloucester County Historical Society: (609) 845-4771

Historical Society of Pennsylvania: (215) 732-6201
Berks County Historical Society: (215) 375-4375
Bucks County Historical Society: (215) 345-0210
(Mercer Museum)
Chadds Ford Historical Society: (215) 388-7376
(Barns-Brinton House)
Chester County Historical Society: (215) 692-4800
(Library, museum, and museum shop open to the public)
Germantown Historical Society: (215) 844-0514
Lancaster County Heritage Center: (717) 299-6440
Lehigh County Historical Society: (215) 435-4664
Marple Newtown Historical Society: (215) 353-3644
(Massey House)
Mennonite Heritage Center: (215) 723-1700
Montgomery County Historic Museum: (215) 272-0297
(museum open weekdays to the public)
New Hope Information Center: (215) 862-5880
(museum open seven days a week)
Radnor Historical Society: (215) 688-2668
(Finley House)
Valley Forge Historical Society: (215) 783-0535

Ethnic Museums

See Museums, page 78.

Religious Museums

See Museums, page 81.

VILLAGES AND HOMESTEADS

Living history beats schoolbooks any day. Most of the villages and homesteads let visitors try their hand at colonial chores. Children begin to understand the difference between today's pets-for-pleasure and old time livestock (raised for food, for wool, for labor, etc.). They learn how hard work was expected from even the youngest members of these homesteads.

Compare the colonial way of life with the Amish lifestyle practiced today. Amish villages and homesteads appear in the Lancaster section, beginning on page 170.

Barclay Farmstead

Barclay Lane
Cherry Hill, NJ 08002
(609) 795-6225

Hours: Mid-January to mid-December, Tuesday and Thursday 1-3:30 PM.

Cost: $1.00 all ages.

Description: 32-acre farm, right in the midst of Cherry Hill, has an operating forge barn, complete with blacksmith shop, corn crib, spring house and restored farmhouse. Ponds and walking trails provide a nice outing.

Time Needed: 1 hour.

Tours/Programs: 45-minute guided tour.

Eating: Picnic tables.

Driving: Cross Ben Franklin Bridge to Rte. 70 east. After second circle, go to first light and take a right on Westgate Drive. Go left at the fork to Barclay Lane.

Codes: 🚐 ⚕

Batsto Village

RD 4, Hammonton, NJ 08037
(609) 561-3262

Hours: Daily, dawn to dusk. Closed Thanksgiving, Christmas and New Year's. Visitor's Center open all year. Summer mansion tours 10 AM-3:30 PM; call in winter.

Cost: Mansion tour $1.50 adults, $.75 children 6-11, under 6 free.

Description: Deep in Wharton State Forest, Batsto Village has almost 20 buildings, well-preserved, from the busy days when it forged cannons and cannon balls for the Revolutionary War. Children enjoy exploring village with its post office, mansion, saw-mill and pens of animals. Stagecoach rides offered Wednesday-Sunday, Memorial Day through Labor Day.

Time Needed: 1 hour mansion tour, 2 hours to see grounds.

Eating: Summer concession stand and picnic area.

Tours/Programs: Available by advance reservation through Wharton State Forest, Batsto Visitor's Center.

Driving: Benjamin Franklin Bridge to New Jersey, follow Rte. 30 into Hammonton. After Kessler Memorial Hospital go left on Rte. 542. Follow signs for Batsto Village 7 miles ahead on left.

Codes: 🚐 ♿

Bridgeton

See Unique Areas page 159.

Before the Dutch settlers arrived, the Lenni-Lenape Indians inhabited the land now called Pennsylvania, New Jersey and Delaware.

Colonial Pennsylvania Plantation

Ridley Creek State Park, Route 3
Media, PA 19063
(215) 566-1725

Hours: April-November, Saturday-Sunday 10 AM-4 PM.
Closed December-March. Open weekdays to school groups
with reservations.

Cost: $2.00 adults, $1.00 under 12.

Description: Enthusiastic costumed guides, both children
and adults, explain the real, often unglamorous way of life of
early American farmhouses. Authentic working farm with
livestock, including piglets in spring. Visitors can try spin-
ning, making cheese, and hauling heavy buckets of water from
the well. Special events regularly scheduled.

Time Needed: 1½ hours to ½ day.

Tours/Programs: School programs let children do chores
from candle dipping to working with animals. Good craft
programs.

Eating: Picnic facilities in Park.

Driving: From Philadelphia, go out Market Street west to
Rte. 3. After you pass Newtown Square, watch for open park on
the left between Rtes. 252 and 352.

Codes: ♿ 🚐 ♟

Conrad Weiser Homestead

RD 1, Womelsdorf, PA 19567
(215) 589-2934

Hours: Wednesday-Saturday 9 AM-5 PM, Sunday 12 Noon-
5 PM. Closed holidays except Memorial Day, July 4, and Labor
Day.

Cost: $1.50 adults, $.50 children 6-17, under 6 free.

Description: This was the farm of colonial Pennsylvania's
"famous treatymaker who kept peace with the Indians on the
frontier." Visit the main house, spring house and gravesite
amidst a beautiful 26-acre park.

Time Needed: 1-2 hours.

Eating: Picnic tables.

Driving: PA Turnpike to Exit 22, to 176 north. Go to Rte. 724
(Phila. Ave.). Follow 724 west to 422 west to Homestead.

Codes: 🚐

Cornwall Furnace

Rexmont Road at Boyd Street, Box 251
Cornwall, PA 17016
(717) 272-9711

Hours: Tuesday-Saturday 9 AM-5 PM, Sunday 12 Noon-5 PM.
OPEN Memorial Day, July 4th, Labor Day.

Cost: $1.50 adults, $.50 children 6-17, under 6 free.

Description: Cornwall's huge furnace produced cannons, munitions and other iron equipment for the Revolutionary War. Watch for the giant coal bins, where trains drove over the bins and dumped their load of charcoal for storage.

Time Needed: 2 hours.

Eating: Picnic tables.

Driving: PA Turnpike west to Exit 20, Rte. 72 north to Quentin. Take a right onto Rte. 419 east, pass Cornwall United Methodist Church. Iron Furnace on right.

Codes: 🚐

Daniel Boone Homestead

RD 2, Box 162
Birdsboro, PA 19508
(215) 582-4900

Hours: Tuesday-Saturday 9 AM-5 PM, Sunday 12 Noon-5 PM.
Closed holidays except Memorial Day, July 4th, Labor Day.

Cost: $1.50 adults, $.50 children 6-17, under 6 free.

Description: Daniel Boone spent his childhood here, learning to trap, shoot and live in the wilderness, until at 16 he left home. See the bank barn, blacksmith shop and sawmill.

Tours/Programs: Bertolet Cabin gives organized groups of young people a chance to "rough it" overnight. Call ahead.

Time Needed: 2 hours.

Eating: Picnic areas located throughout property. The one we liked best lies between sawmill and lodge.

Driving: I-76 west, Rte. 202 south to Rte. 422 west past Pottstown. When road is split by median strip, watch for signs and turn right on Daniel Boone Road, then left on Homestead driveway. Go past lodge to main house.

Codes: ♿ 🍽 🚐

Historic Fallsington, Inc.

4 Yardley Avenue
Fallsington, PA 19054
(215) 295-6567

Hours: March 15-November 15, Wednesday-Sunday 11 AM-4 PM.

Cost: $2.50 adults, $1.00 children 6-18, under 6 free.

Description: See how village developed over three centuries. Go from a 17th-century log cabin to lovely 18th-century houses, to 19th-century Victorian extravaganzas. Religious life centered around four Friends Meeting Houses.

Time Needed: 1 hour.

Tours/Programs: Must take tour to go into buildings; see audio/visual program in headquarters.

Eating: Picnic area.

Driving: PA Turnpike east to Exit 29, north on Rte. 13 for 5 miles. Left onto Tyburn Road, right at light onto New Falls Road. Go ½ mile to main on Meetinghouse Square.

Codes: ♿ 🚌 ♀

Hopewell Furnace and Village

RD 1, Box 345
Elverson, PA 19520
(215) 582-8773

Hours: Daily 9 AM-5 PM. Closed Christmas and New Year's.

Cost: $1.00 adults, $3.00 family, under 12 free.

Description: See how a 1777 iron plantation operated: explore the homes of the iron workers, the luxurious home of the ironmaster, the furnace, charcoal house, blacksmith's house, cooling shed. Self-guided walking tour begins at the Visitor's Center after your choice of an orientation slide show, videos, or just a chat with the ranger.

Time Needed: 2 hours. Lots of walking!

Tours/Programs: Living history program in July and August with costumed blacksmiths, carpenters and cooks at work.

Eating: Picnic at French Creek State Park.

Driving: PA Turnpike west to exit 22. Take Rte. 100 north, Rte. 23 west, Rte. 345 north. Watch for signs.

Codes: ♿ 🚌

Newlin Grist Mill Park

Box 219, South Cheyney Road
Glen Mills, PA 19342
(215) 459-2359

Hours: Daily 8 AM-dusk.

Cost: Free; fee for fishing.

Description: Most children make a beeline for the stocked stream fishing. Mill and miller's house, blacksmith shop, spring house, small log cabin reception center offer insight into the Mill's original purpose.

Eating: Picnic groves in woods and along the stream are very popular—reservations recommended.

Driving: Rte. 1 south through Media. Seven miles past Media, go left on South Cheyney Road. Mill is on your left.

Codes: ♿ 🚐

Pusey House and Landingford Plantation

15 Race Street, Upland, PA 19015
(215) 874-5665

Hours: May 1-September 15, Saturday and Sunday 1-4 PM.

Cost: $1.00 adults, $.75 children and students.

Description: Caleb Pusey's house was built in 1683 and has been preserved in its original condition. See large kettle (probably used to dye clothes or brew beer), beehive oven, the well inside the house, and a candlestick used for candles or for removing pig bristles after the animals were slaughtered.

Time Needed: ½ hour to 1 hour.

Tours/Programs: Frequent programs throughout the year.

Eating: Picnic area.

Driving: I-95 south to Widener University Exit in Chester. Turn right off ramp, then left onto 14th Street, which turns into Upland Avenue. Pass Chester-Crozier Medical Center on Upland, turn right on 6th, then left on Main. Follow bend which leads to Race Street.

Codes: 🚐

Smithville

Mount Holly, NJ 08060
(609) 265-5068

Hours: April-November, Wednesday 10 AM-3 PM, Sunday 1-4 PM.

Cost: $2.50 adults, $2.00 students, under 6 free.

Description: This town was so complete it even had, in 1892, a bicycle commuter railway connecting it to nearby Mount Holly (the H.B. Smith Company invented a kerosene-burning tricycle and the high-wheeled Star bicycle). In the 1840 mansion, see children's room, doll collection and children's tram.

Time Needed: 1 hour for tour.

Tours/Programs: Tour features Orientation/Exhibit Center, Victorian House Museum, Casino Annex/Art Gallery, gardens and grounds. Guides can adjust tour for children.

Driving: From Philadelphia, take the Benjamin Franklin Bridge to Rte. 70 east to Rte. 38 east to Rte. 530. Go left on Rte. 681 north, then watch for the mansion on your left.

Codes: ♿ 🚐 ⚡

Wentz Farmstead

P.O. Box 240, Worcester, PA 19490
(215) 584-5104

Hours: Tuesday-Saturday 10 AM-4 PM, Sunday 1-4 PM. Closed Mondays and major holidays.

Cost: Free, donations appreciated.

Description: Brief slide show in Peter Wentz Reception Center introduces visitors to this carefully reconstructed working farm. Livestock, growing crops, and guides in costume lend authenticity. Children love the kitchen and the children's bedroom, where blankets were warmed for the night on a special chimney ledge.

Time Needed: 1 hour house tour; allow more time for outside.

Programs: Many excellent programs where craftspeople show how to make 18th-century household items using original tools. Summer colonial crafts camp for children.

Driving: I-76 west, Rte. 202 south, Rte. 422 west, Rte. 363 north. Follow Rte. 363 north for approximately 10 miles. Cross Skippack Pike and watch for signs.

Codes: ♿ 🍴 🚐 ⚡

Wheaton Village

Millville, NJ 08032
(609) 825-6800

Hours: April-December, daily 10 AM-5 PM; January-March, call for hours. Closed major holidays.

Cost: $9.00 family, $4.00 adults, $2.00 students, under 5 free.

Description: Watch glass blowers at work in 1888 glass factory still in full use. Museum of American Glass has more than 7,000 pieces. Half-scale railroad takes visitors on a ¾ mile trip around Village grounds. Youngest children enjoy playground and lakeside. Older ones watch tinsmiths at work and see fully equipped turn-of-the-century printing business.

Time Needed: 2 hours.

Tours/Programs: Glass blowing demonstrations at 11 AM, 1:30 and 3:30 PM. Artists' demonstrations and special events like Woodcarver's Show throughout the year.

Eating: Cafeteria open daily April-December.

Driving: Cross Ben Franklin or Walt Whitman Bridge from Philadelphia into New Jersey to I-676 south, to Rte. 42 south, to Rte. 55 south (it all happens quickly). Stay on Rte. 55 for 1 hour to Rte. 47 south. Turn right on Main Street (Rte. 49 west) then follow signs for Village.

Codes: 👯 ☂ 🚐 👦

New Jersey is the 46th largest state and could fit into Texas 37 times.

Museums

Mummers Museum, train museums, doll museums, soldier and war museums, natural history museums, art and science museums—there are enough in this area to delight a child with a different museum every weekend for almost two full years! The Please Touch Museum is designed JUST for children seven and under. The Allentown Art Museum and the Mercer Museum are well worth the drive, wherever you live.

A number of outstanding museums are not listed out of respect for their exclusivity. The Barnes Foundation Art Collection for instance is one of our favorite museums, but since it does not admit children under 12 years old, it is not included here.

Academy of Natural Sciences

19th Street and the Parkway
Philadelphia, PA 19103
(215) 299-1000

Hours: Monday-Friday 10 AM-4 PM, Saturday, Sunday and some holidays, 10 AM-5 PM. Closed Thanksgiving, Christmas and New Year's.

Cost: $4.50 adults, $3.50 children 3-12, under 3 free. Group rates for 10 or more people.

Description: Home of everyone's favorite full-scale roaring dinosaur. "Discovering Dinosaurs" is an exciting, multi-media approach to the beasts with lots of games to play and buttons to push. "Outside-In" is the museum's special third floor children's nature area where they can explore habitats, play with small animals and stay busy. Intriguing dioramas.
Time Needed: 2 hours.

Tours/Programs: Outstanding programs using live animals help children ages 3 and over better understand the animal kingdom.

Eating: "The Eatery" has tables and vending machines.

Codes: ♿ ⛲ 🚐 👪 🍴

Allentown Art Museum

31 North Fifth Street, P.O. Box 117
Allentown, PA 18105
(215) 432-4333

Hours: Tuesday-Saturday 10 AM-5 PM, Sunday 1-5 PM.

Cost: Free, but voluntary contributions requested.

Description: Small and friendly—a perfect art museum for children. Max Hess Junior Gallery has art to see, touch, hear, climb through, and play with. Ask for Kids Treasure Hunt pamphlet. Older children enjoy Frank Lloyd Wright Room and a chance to search for his red square trademark.
Time Needed: 1 hour.

Tours/Programs: Many children's programs through the year.

Driving: PA Turnpike to Northeast Extension to Lehigh Valley Exit 33. Follow Rte. 22 east to 7th St. Turn right on 7th, left on Turner for two blocks, then right onto 5th. Museum is 1½ blocks ahead on the left, behind the courthouse.

Codes: ♿ ⛲ 🚐 👪 🍴

Atwater Kent Museum

15 South 7th Street
Philadelphia, PA 19106
(215) 686-3630, or 922-3031

Hours: Tuesday-Saturday 9:30 AM-4:45 PM.

Cost: Free.

Description: Treasures and trivia of old Philadelphia abound. Artifacts, maps, paintings, prints and photographs reflect the city's social and cultural history. Look for antique toy collection on the second floor.

Codes: 🚶 👕 🚐 ♿

Balch Institute

See Ethnic Museums, page 78.

Boyertown Museum of Historic Vehicles

28 Warwick Street
Boyertown, PA 19512
(215) 367-2090

Hours: Tuesday-Friday 8 AM-4 PM, Saturday-Sunday 10 AM-2 PM.

Cost: $2.50 adults, $1.50 students, under 6 free.

Description: There are more than 100 different vehicles here from old sleighs to butcher's wagons, to large-wheel bicycles— all built in Southeastern Pennsylvania. Boyertown-to-Reading stagecoach, fire equipment and a number of Charles Duryea's Reading automobiles add to the pride and feeling for local heritage.

Time Needed: 1-2 hours.

Driving: I-76 (Schuylkill Expressway) west, Rte. 202 south, Rte. 422 west to Rte. 100 north at Pottstown, to Boyertown Exit. Go left onto Rte. 73. At 5th light turn left onto Reading Avenue. At the fork go straight (road bears to the right). Museum parking lot ahead on the right.

Codes: 🚶 👕 🚐 ♿

Brandywine River Museum

Route 1, Chadds Ford, PA 19317
(215) 459-1900, or 388-7601

Hours: Daily 9:30 AM-4:30 PM. Closed Christmas Day.

Cost: $3.00 adults, $1.50 children 6-12, under 6 free.

Description: An indoor-outdoor museum, focusing on the beautiful Brandywine Valley and the museum's adjacent nature preserve. Old grist mill museum displays naturalistic paintings by Wyeths and their compatriots. Rugged book illustrations appeal to older children who know the stories of Robin Hood, Treasure Island, etc. Even the youngest children love the cobblestone courtyard and interior ramps.

Time Needed: 1½ hours.

Tours/Programs: Children of all ages love the annual holiday train display and see the giant Christmas trees decorated with natural materials from the surrounding woods and fields. Many interesting programs and shows all year 'round.

Eating: Restaurant in museum.

Driving: I-95 south to 322 north to Rte. 1 south. After crossing Rte. 100 in Chadds Ford, watch for museum on left.

Codes: 👟 ⛪ 🚐 ♿

Buten Museum

246 North Bowman Avenue
Merion, PA 19066
(215) 664-6601

Hours: Monday-Friday 2-4 PM.

Cost: $2.50 adults, $1.00 children under 16.

Description: Collection of Wedgewood porcelain as few have ever seen it. Appropriate for older students of ceramics.

Driving: I-76 (Schuylkill Expressway) west to City Avenue Exit (Rte. 1). Follow City Avenue south for about one mile to Old Lancaster Road on right (the street is called 58th Street on the left). Go right on Old Lancaster to 2nd traffic light, left onto Montgomery Avenue, Bowman is 2nd small street on right. Museum is 2nd house on right after turn onto Bowman.

Codes: ⛪ 🚐

Campbell Museum

Campbell Place
Camden, NJ 08101
(609) 342-6440

Hours: Monday-Friday 9 AM-4:30 PM.

Cost: Free.

Description: Extraordinary collection of soup tureens and bowls, some dating as far back as 3000 B.C.! Be sure to look for the Frog Tureen and the Four Paw Soup Tureen Menagerie. Call ahead to arrange to see 20-minute film.

Driving: Ben Franklin Bridge straight to I-676. Stay in right lane and follow signs for Campbell Place. Museum straight ahead.

Codes:

Choo-Choo Barn

See Lancaster, page 172.

Cigna Museum

1600-1700 Arch Street
Philadelphia, PA 19103
(215) 523-4894

Hours: Museum and Gallery: Monday-Friday 9 AM-5 PM. Lobby Exhibits: Monday-Friday 8 AM-6 PM.

Cost: Free.

Description: The importance of sea trade in early Philadelphia is evident in this insurance company's collection of marine artifacts, paintings, models and prints. Early volunteer fire company equipment, clothing, inventions and related paraphernalia like fire marks appeal to all children.

Time Needed: 1 hour.

Codes:

New Jersey had its own "Tea Party" on the eve of the Revolutionary War, December 12, 1774.

Colonial Flying Corps Museum

New Garden Airport, Newark Road
Toughkenamon, PA 19374
(215) 268-2048, or 268-8988

Hours: May through September, Saturday-Sunday 12 Noon-4 PM. Closed in inclement weather; call before you go.

Cost: $1.00 adults, $.50 children under 12.

Description: Small but interesting collection of antique airplanes, motorcycles and cars. Someone always on duty to answer questions about classics such as 1929 DuPont auto, Indian motorcycles from 1907 to 1952, Staggerwing Beech and Grummen Wildcat planes.

Time Needed: 1 hour.

Eating: Picnic tables, snack bar in airport.

Driving: I-95 south to Rte. 322 north to Rte. 1 south to Kennett Square Bypass to Toughkenamon Exit. Go left onto Newark Road. Museum is two miles ahead on the right.

Codes: 👩‍🦽 ✈

Delaware Art Museum

2301 Kentmere Parkway
Wilmington, DE 19806
(302) 571-9590

Hours: Tuesday 10 AM-9 PM, Wednesday-Saturday 10 AM-5 PM, Sunday 12 Noon-5 PM. Children's Gallery closes at 4 PM each day. Closed Thanksgiving, Christmas and New Year's.

Cost: Free, donation requested.

Description: "Pegofoamasaurus" Children's Gallery starts right, with welcoming doors for every size person. Peg-covered walls for children to create their own art with infinitely different shapes and colors of foam. Check ahead on weekdays so your visit won't conflict with school groups.

Time Needed: 1 hour.

Eating: Field next to parking lot is good for picnics.

Driving: I-95 south to Rte. 52 Delaware Avenue Exit 7. Go right at the first light onto Pennsylvania Avenue. Bear right where the road splits. Go two miles, then right onto Bancroft Parkway to dead end. Go left onto Kentmere Parkway. Museum is on right.

Codes: 👩‍🦽 ✈ 🚌 🎧

Delaware County Institute of Science

11 Veterans Square
Media, PA 19063
(215) 566-3491

Hours: Monday 9 AM-1 PM, Thursday 9 AM-12 Noon.

Cost: Free.

Description: Minerals, flora, fauna and maps of Delaware County.

Driving: Rte. 1 south from Philadelphia to Media bypass. Take bypass and get off at Providence Road (Rte. 252). Follow Rte. 252 south into Media. At trolley tracks, go right onto State Street, then right at Veterans Square. Institute is ½ block ahead on the right.

Codes: 🛝 🚐

Delaware Museum of Natural History

P.O. Box 3937
Wilmington, DE 19807
(302) 652-7600 recorded, or 658-9111

Hours: Monday-Saturday 9:30 AM-4:30 PM, Sunday 12 Noon-5 PM. Closed July 4, Thanksgiving, Christmas, New Year's.

Cost: $2.50 adults, $1.75 students under 21 and children 6-16, under 6 free.

Description: Here you truly float through land, water and air. "Land" exhibit focuses on mammals found in Delaware; "Water" uses incredible shell collection and treasures to recreate the Great Barrier Reef. In "Air", watch for those huge, scary birds of prey perched above you in the trees.

Time Needed: 2 hours.

Tours/Programs: Discovery Room, open on weekends and for special events, has many hands-on activities. Weekend films and workshops presented all year 'round. Spring and winter Children's Weeks offer special events.

Driving: I-95 south from Philadelphia to Rte. 52 Delaware Avenue Exit 7. Museum is 10 miles ahead on the left, two miles past the town of Greenville.

Codes: ♿ 🛝 🚐 🍴

Drexel University Museum Collection

Main Building, Room 305
32nd and Chestnut Streets
Philadelphia, PA 19104
(215) 895-2424

Hours: Monday-Friday 1-4 PM.

Cost: Free.

Description: Antique American and European furniture, antique toys, porcelain, 19th-century art, portraits of Drexel family.

Codes: 👤🎭🚐

Elfreth's Alley Museum

See Glimpses of History, page 29.

Fireman's Hall Museum

Second and Quarry Streets
Philadelphia, PA 19106
(215) 922-9844

Hours: Tuesday-Saturday 9 AM-5 PM. Closed major holidays.

Cost: Free.

Description: The authentic 1815 Hand Pumper appeals to the imagination, but young minds find earlier firefighting equipment totally incredible. Hand-sewn leather buckets and crude hatchets don't LOOK like much until they're seen in pictures of community bucket brigades. Ben Franklin started the first fire company in 1736. Equipment through the ages, firemarks, and recreated Fireman's Living Quarters give visitors plenty to see in this original firehouse.

Time Needed: 1 hour.

Codes: 👤🎭

The capital of
Delaware is Dover.

First Pennsylvania Bank Museum

Center Square West
16th and Market Streets
Philadelphia, PA 19107
(215) 786-8420

Hours: Monday-Friday 9 AM-5 PM. Closed bank holidays.

Cost: Free.

Description: America's oldest commercial bank displays an authentic reproduction of the bank's first business office.

Codes: &

Folk Craft Center and Museum

See Lancaster, page 174.

Fonthill Museum

East Court Street
Doylestown, PA 18901
(215) 348-9461

Hours: Monday-Sunday 10 AM-5 PM. Closed Thanksgiving, Christmas and New Year's.

Cost: $3.00 adults, $1.50 students.

Description: Henry Mercer built Fonthill for his collection of prints and tiles from around the world. Even children with no interest in ceramics are fascinated by the medieval castle-like atmosphere of this VERY unusual house. Further down the driveway, visit Mercer's Moravian Pottery and Tile Works (page 189) and the Mercer Museum (page 64).

Time Needed: 45 minutes for guided tour.

Eating: Picnic area in Fonthill Park.

Driving: PA Turnpike to exit 27. Follow Rte. 611 north through Doylestown, and turn right on East Court Street. Watch for signs.

Codes: & ⛑ 🚐 ♿

Pennsylvania's nicknames are the Quaker State and the Keystone State.

Franklin Institute Science Museum and Fels Planetarium

20th Street and Ben Franklin Parkway
Philadelphia, PA 19103
(215) 564-3375 recorded, or 448-1200

Hours: Monday-Saturday 10 AM-5 PM, Sunday 12 Noon-5 PM. Closed major holidays.

Cost: $4.50 adults, $3.00 senior citizens, $3.50 children 4-11, under 4 free.

Description: Do-it-yourself discovery displays for all ages. Communications Exhibit lets you see yourself on TV, operate a telephone switchboard, learn how TV and radio work, learn about printing and paper, and much more. Take a short train ride in a real engine, see how the camera was invented. Children's planetarium show at 10:30 AM on Saturday (the only time youngsters under 4 are allowed in planetarium).

Time Needed: 2-3 hours.

Tours/Programs: Frequent programs throughout the year; check for those geared to children, such as Slim Goodbody Show. School and group tours, arranged in advance to coincide with studies, are excellent. Haunted House at Halloween, Flashlight Holiday Concert in December.

Eating: Fast food cafeteria; many street vendors outside.

Codes: ♿ ⛟ 🚐 ♺

Franklin Mint

Route 1, Baltimore Pike
Franklin Center, PA 19063
(215) 459-6168

Hours: Tuesday-Saturday 9:30 AM-4:30 PM, Sunday 1-4:30 PM. Closed holidays.

Cost: Free.

Description: Large, well-designed display of pewter, bronze, coins, porcelain and collectibles.

Driving: Rte. 1 south from Philadelphia. After Media, watch for Franklin Center on your left.

Codes: ♿ ⛟ 🚐

Gast Classic Motor Cars Exhibit

See Lancaster, page 174.

Glencairn Museum

1001 Papermill Road
Bryn Athyn, PA 19009
(215) 947-9919

Hours: Weekdays 9 AM-5 PM by reservation only for tours.
Open without tours second Sunday of every month.

Cost: $3.00 adults, under 12 free.

Description: Young history students have plenty to see in
this unusual collection of art and objects arranged in galleries
by subject, including Greece and Rome, Near East and Far
East, Middle Ages, American Indian and French art.

Tours/Programs: 2-hour guided tour.

Driving: Directions given with reservations.

Codes: &.🛈 🚐

Hall of Fame Sports Museum

See Bridgeton, page 160.

Hershey Museum

See Hershey, page 169.

Historic Burlington County Prison-Museum

128 High Street
Mount Holly, NJ 08060
(609) 265-5958

Hours: April-November, Wednesday 10 AM-12 Noon and
1-4 PM. Saturday by appointment only.

Cost: Free, donations appreciated.

Description: This prison, where both a Supreme Court jus-
tice and the Boston Strangler have been jailed, was built in
1811 and used till 1965. Tour explains its history and includes
some exciting stories of prison life. See their cells, each with
fireplace and window. The "dungeon" is said to be haunted!
First fireproof building in the U.S.

Time Needed: 1 hour for tour, often given by "Charlie," a Cor-
rection Officer at the prison before it closed.

Driving: Ben Franklin Bridge to New Jersey, I-295 north to
Mt. Holly Exit. Follow Rte. 38 east to Mt. Holly Bypass (Rte. 541
north), go right at first light, left at second light onto High
Street. Museum is 1½ blocks on the right.

Codes: 🛈 🚐 👤

Historical Society of Pennsylvania

1300 Locust Street
Philadelphia 19107
(215) 732-6200

Hours: Tuesday-Friday 9 AM-5 PM, Saturday 10 AM-3 PM.

Cost: Free.

Description: Main exhibit hall has shows that change several times a year, using artifacts from their incredible collection of bits of Pennsylvaniana. Joint shows are arranged occasionally with neighboring Library Company.

Codes: ♿ ✝ 🚐

Institute of Contemporary Art

The University of Pennsylvania
34th and Walnut Streets
Philadelphia, PA 19104
(215) 898-5118, or 898-7108

Hours: Daily 10 AM-5 PM; Wednesday and Friday, open till 8 PM.

Cost: Free, suggested contribution.

Description: Four major exhibits shown during the school year. Workshops for 5- to 12-year-olds every weekend during school year.

Codes: ♿ ✝ 🚐

La Salle University Art Museum

20th and Olney Avenue
Philadelphia, PA 19141
(215) 951-1221

Hours: Tuesday-Friday 11 AM-4 PM, Sunday 2-4 PM.

Cost: Free.

Description: Collection of paintings, prints and drawings arranged to document Western Art since the Middle Ages.

Codes: ♿ ✝ 🚐 ⚲

Mary Merritt Doll Museum and Merritt's Museum of Childhood

RD 2, Route 422
Douglassville, PA 19518
(215) 385-3809 and 385-3408

Hours: Monday-Saturday 10 AM-5 PM, Sunday 1-5 PM. Closed major holidays, open others 11 AM-5 PM.

Cost: $2.00 adults, $1.00 children 5-12, under 5 free. Admission to both museums included in price.

Description: The Doll Museum: great collection of dolls, dollhouses, Noah's Arks. Museum of Childhood: one-room exhibit of childhood mementos, dollhouses, banks, Indian artifacts, sleighs, costumes and a full-sized handcarved canoe.

Time Needed: 1-2 hours.

Driving: I-76 (Schuylkill Expressway) west to Rte. 202 south to Rte. 422 west. Museum on the right beyond Pottstown.

Codes: 👟 🎠 🚐

Mercer Mile

See Mercer Museum, below; Fonthill, page 60, and Moravian Pottery and Tile Works, page 189.

Mercer Museum and Spruance Library

Pine and Ashland Streets
Doylestown, PA 18901
(215) 345-0210

Hours: Monday-Saturday 10 AM-5 PM, Sunday 1-5 PM. Closed Thanksgiving, Christmas, January and February.

Cost: $3.00 adults, $1.50 students, under 6 free.

Description: Intriguing castle-like museum with displays that you walk over, under and around. Tools used by early Americans range from beehive oven to gallows. Discover a hurdy-gurdy, a cloverheader, a snairing and a sausage stuffer. See shops of a hatter, baker, lumberman, basket and broom maker, and an old school. Clock making, gun smithing, glass blowing.

Time Needed: 2 hours to a full day.

Programs: Many fun programs, including summer camp.

Driving: PA Turnpike to Exit 27, Rte. 611 north to Doylestown. Cross Rte. 202; at light take a *sharp* right on Green Street. Museum is on the left.

Codes: 👟 🎠 🚐 🎒

Mummers Museum

2nd and Washington Avenue
Philadelphia, PA 19147
(215) 336-3050

Hours: Tuesday-Saturday 9:30 AM-5 PM, Sunday 12 Noon-5 PM. Closed Mondays except legal holidays, Thanksgiving, Christmas, and New Year's.

Cost: $1.50 adults, $.75 under 12.

Description: Just as much fun as the famous Mummer's Parade! Full of sights and sounds to get feet moving, including video instructions on how to do the Mummers Strut.

Time Needed: 1 hour.

Codes:

Museum of the Philadelphia Civic Center

34th Street and Civic Center Boulevard
Philadelphia, PA 19104
(215) 823-7206, or 823-7243

Description: Open October-June for school groups only. No fees. Teachers can request areas to be discussed using Museum's collection: local government, anthropology, geography and the environment, and everything in between.

Mutter Museum of the College of Physicians

19 South 22nd Street
Philadelphia, PA 19103
(215) 561-6050, ext. 41

Hours: Tuesday-Friday 10 AM-4 PM.

Cost: Free.

Description: Skeletons and old medical equipment are just a few of the items in the history of medicine and treatment center.

Codes:

Nail House Museum

See Bridgeton, page 160.

National Archives-Philadelphia Branch

Room 1350, 9th and Market Streets
Philadelphia, PA 19107
(215) 597-3000

Hours: Monday-Friday 8 AM-5 PM, first and third Saturday
of the month, 8 AM-Noon.

Cost: Free.

Description: Official documents, such as Civil War records
and passenger lists from all boats that arrived in Philadelphia
from 1800 to 1948, are filed away but the Museum gives a good
idea of their scope.

Codes: ♿ 🦌 🚐

National Wax Museum

See Lancaster, page 176.

New Jersey State Museum and Planetarium

205 West State Street
Trenton, NJ 08608
(609) 292-6308

Hours: Monday-Saturday 9 AM-4:45 PM, Sunday 1-5 PM.
Closed major holidays.

Cost: Free.

Description: Everything under one roof. Weekends visit the
planetarium and Delaware Valley Indian displays. See North
American Mammals, reptiles, and the Hadrosaurus, "first
dinosaur in North America, found in Haddonfield, NJ . . . hence
the name." Hall of Natural Science shows how the earth was
3000 million years ago, how it is today, and how it might be in
the future. Also galleries of paintings, sculpture and other
arts.

Time Needed: 2 hours to ½ day.

Driving: Ben Franklin Bridge to NJ, follow signs to I-295
north to Rte. 130 north to Rte. 206 north. Left on Laylor Street
to Rte. 29. Go right on Rte. 29 to Willow Street. Bear left, go ¾
way around War Memorial Building. At light go straight into
parking lot.

Codes: ♿ 🦌 🚐 🛝

Newcomen Library and Museum

412 Newcomen Road
Exton, PA 19341
(215) 363-6600

Hours: Monday-Friday 9 AM-5 PM, weekends by appointment.

Cost: Free, donations appreciated.

Description: Great collection of artifacts, books, and working models related to steam technology and industrial history. Recommended for children over age 5 who can appreciate complexity of machines and delicacy of instruments.

Time Needed: 1 hour.

Tours/Programs: Enthusiastic staff will answer any questions. Group tours by arrangement.

Eating: None, but picnics possible on lawn.

Driving: Rte. 30 west from Philadelphia. Go through Paoli, pass Rte. 202, go right on Ship Road. Go 1.8 miles to the 4th street on the right, Newcomen Museum is ahead on the right .2 miles.

Codes: 🦽 ⛪ 🚐 ⚘

Norman Rockwell Museum

6th and Sansom Streets (in Curtis Publishing Building)
Philadelphia, PA 19106
(215) 922-4345

Hours: Daily 10 AM-4 PM. Closed Thanksgiving, Christmas, New Year's.

Cost: $1.50, under 12 free.

Description: Children see their friends in the situations drawn by Rockwell, but never themselves! Rockwell walked to work in this building where the old Saturday Evening Post was published. Museum includes a replica of the artist's studio. Lots of young boys (Rockwell had three sons), not many girls, but situations universal to all families.

Time Needed: 1 hour.

Tours/Programs: Tours available by arrangement.

Codes: 🦽 ⛪ 🚐

North Museum of Franklin and Marshall College

See Lancaster, page 177.

Old Barracks Museum

Barrack Street
Trenton, NJ 08608
(609) 396-1776

Hours: Monday-Saturday 10 AM-5 PM, Sunday 1-5 PM. Closed Thanksgiving, Christmas, New Year's and Easter.

Cost: Suggested donation: $1.00 adults, $.50 children 12 and under.

Description: There are only 5 wartime barracks left in the United States. This was built to house soldiers during the French and Indian Wars (1689-1763). If you're curious, talk to some of the soldiers about their life there; role-playing guides make the difficulties of barracks life very clear! 300 men plus women and children lived together here. The women were allowed half-rations for themselves and their children, in exchange for cooking, cleaning and sewing.

Time Needed: ½ to 1 hour.

Driving: Ben Franklin Bridge to I-295 north to Rte. 130 north to Rte. 206 north (South Broad Street) to Laylor Street. Go left on Laylor Street, follow signs to Rte. 29 North to Barrack Street.

Codes: 👨‍🦽 ⛱ 🚐 ☕

Peale House

1820 Chestnut Street
Philadelphia, PA 19103
(215) 569-2797

Hours: Tuesday-Saturday 10 AM-4 PM, Sunday 12 Noon-4 PM.

Cost: Free.

Description: Branch gallery of the Pennsylvania Academy of Fine Arts. Changing exhibits and some student work.

Codes: 👨‍🦽 ⛱ 🚐

Pennsylvania Academy of the Fine Arts

Broad and Cherry Streets
Philadelphia, PA 19102
(215) 972-7633 recorded, or 972-7600

Hours: Tuesday-Saturday 10 AM-5 PM, Sunday 11 AM-5 PM.

Cost: $3.00 adults, $2.00 children and senior citizens.

Description: The combination of museum and school makes a visit here an enjoyable learning experience. Manageable size with changing exhibits from the Museum's outstanding American collection. Look at the building from the outside, too!

Time Needed: 1-2 hours.

Tours/Programs: Family programs once a month; summer arts camp.

Codes: 👤🐦🚐

Pennsylvania Hospital and Nursing Museum

8th and Spruce Streets
Philadelphia, PA 19107
(215) 829-3971

Hours: Daily 9 AM-4 PM.

Cost: Free.

Description: Half-hour tour includes history of hospital, early medical instruments, history of Nursing Museum, and first surgical amphitheater (built 1804) in the country.

Codes: 👤

Perelman Antique Toy Museum

270 South Second Street
Philadelphia, PA 19106
(215) WA 2-1070

Hours: Daily 9:30 AM-5 PM.

Cost: $2.00 adults, $.95 children under 14.

Description: Sophisticated antique toys, such as mechanical banks and animated cap pistols, are now collectors' items. Mostly tin and cast-iron, the intriguing toys instill wonder and occasionally frustration at not being allowed to touch.

Time Needed: 1 hour.

Codes: 👤🐦🚐

Philadelphia Art Alliance

251 South 18th Street
Philadelphia, PA 19103
(215) 545-4302

Hours: Monday, Friday, Saturday, 10:30-5 PM; Tuesday, Wednesday, Thursday, 10:30-9 PM.

Cost: Free.

Description: Stately home on Rittenhouse Square houses seven galleries of changing exhibits of arts and crafts. Programs for children one Saturday each month range from cartoon workshop to poetry workshop to T-shirt making.

Codes: 🎭

Philadelphia Maritime Museum

321 Chestnut Street
Philadelphia, PA 19106
(215) 925-5439

Hours: Monday-Saturday 10 AM-5 PM, Sunday 1-5 PM. Closed major holidays.

Cost: Free, donation appreciated.

Description: Ship models, scrimshaw, items from the Titanic, fishing implements and navigational instruments are just a few of the treasures. Museum pays tribute to the heritage of Philadelphia as a busy seaport. Library open by appointment.

Time Needed: 1 hour.

Codes: ♿ 🎭 🚐 ♫

Philadelphia Maritime Museum's Workshop on the Water

Boat Basin at Penn's Landing
Philadelphia, PA 19106
(215) 925-7589

Hours: Wednesday-Sunday 9:30 AM-4:30 PM. Closed holidays.

Cost: Free, donation appreciated.

Description: A real, boat-building workshop. Not easily understood by the very young, but fascinating for older children who have tried to make models or work with wood.

Time Needed: ½ hour.

Eating: None, but many places nearby on Penn's Landing.

Codes: 🎭 🚐

Philadelphia Museum of Art

26th Street and Ben Franklin Parkway, PO Box 7646
Philadelphia, PA 19101
(215) 763-8100, or 787-5488 daily events recording.

Hours: Tuesday 11 AM-3 PM (hourly guided tours only),
Wednesday-Sunday 10 AM-5 PM. Closed Mondays and
holidays.

Cost: $4.00 adults, $2.00 5-year-olds through college students. Free on Sundays, 10 AM-1 PM, pay whatever you wish
on Tuesdays.

Description: It would take pages to list all the fine features of
the Philadelphia Museum of Art. Children seem eagerly
attracted to the Indian temple and arms and armory exhibits.
Young children do well with the workbook *Let's Go to the Art
Museum*, available in the Museum Shop.

Time Needed: As long as a child's interest lasts.

Tours/Programs: Year 'round family programs, films, lectures, tours, special performances and children's activities.

Eating: Cafeteria and restaurant.

Codes: 👤 ✈ 🚐 ♫

Phillips Mushroom Museum

Route 1
Kennett Square, PA 19348
(215) 388-6082

Hours: Daily 10 AM-6 PM.

Cost: $1.25 adults, $.75 senior citizens, $.50 children 7-12,
under 6 free.

Description: Small exhibit and movie shows process of cultivating mushrooms. See real mushrooms growing.

Driving: Rte. 1 south from Philadelphia; watch for small
museum on your right after Media.

Codes: 👤 ✈ 🚐

The state tree of Delaware
is the American holly.

Please Touch Museum

210 North 21st Street
Philadelphia, PA 19103
(215) 963-0666   (963-0667 for current activities)

Hours: Tuesday-Sunday 10 AM-4:30 PM. Closed Mondays and holidays.

Cost: $4.00 per person.

Description: Designed on the theory that we all learn best by doing, Please Touch is the only museum in the country just for children ages 7 and under—but it has plenty to entertain the whole family. Be a doctor and try out the equipment in the Health Care Center, dress up in foreign costumes, explore the calliope exhibit about musical sounds. Ride a trolley like the one on "Mr. Rogers' Neighborhood."

Resource Center offers individual activities: examine fossils, then do stone rubbings. Virginia Evans Theater schedules mime, puppets, poetry, storytelling for all ages.

Time Needed: 1-2 hours.

Tours/Programs: Films, parent-child workshops and outstanding special events throughout the year (*see* Calendar of Events, pages 197-204).

Eating: A room for bring-your-own picnics.

Codes: 👤 🌳 🚌 👥 🖼
Note: strollers not permitted on the gallery floor.

Port of History Museum

At Penn's Landing
Delaware Avenue and Walnut Street
Philadelphia, PA 19106
(215) 925-3804

Hours: Wednesday-Sunday 8:30 AM-4:30 PM.

Cost: $2.00 adults, $1.00 children.

Description: 40 ship models in the permanent collection, plus changing exhibits. Theater for group performances.

Eating: Many vendors outside.

Codes: 👤 🌳 🚌 👥

Railroad Museum of Pennsylvania

See Lancaster, page 179.

Reading Public Museum and Art Gallery

500 Museum Road
Reading, PA 19611
(215) 371-5850

Hours: Monday-Friday 9 AM-5 PM, Saturday 1-4 PM, Sunday 1-5 PM. Closed holidays.

Cost: Donation requested: $1.00 adults, $.50 children.

Description: First floor exhibits of birds, Indians, prehistoric fossils and minerals. Area on Eastern cultures, ancient civilizations, South Seas and armor. Second floor has art gallery with changing exhibits. Planetarium for groups only.

Time Needed: 1-2 hours.

Tours/Programs: Plenty of tours and programs for children of all ages. Museum is part of school system.

Eating: Playground across the street is possible for picnics.

Driving: I-76 (Schuylkill Expressway) west to Rte. 202 south to Rte. 422 north into Reading. Go through the center of the city, over Penn Street Bridge, then three more blocks to Fifth Avenue. Left on Fifth Avenue which turns into Museum Road. Museum is on right.

Codes: 👟 🚌 🏕

Rodin Museum

22nd Street and Ben Franklin Parkway
Philadelphia, PA 19101
(215) 763-8100

Hours: Tuesday-Sunday 10 AM-5 PM. Closed holidays.

Cost: Free, donation requested.

Description: Anyone familiar with the French sculptor's beautiful work is delighted with Philadelphia's own collection, the largest outside Paris.

Codes: 👟 🚌

Rosenbach Museum and Library

2010 Delancey Place
Philadelphia, PA 19103
(215) 732-1600

Hours: Tuesday-Sunday 11 AM-4 PM.

Cost: $2.50 house tour, $1.50 exhibit only, $1.50 children
and senior citizens.

Description: Maurice Sendak collection is most readily rec-
ognized by children and explains book illustration from concept to finished product. As dealers and collectors, the
Rosenbach brothers gathered drawings, paintings and artifacts of literary figures and original manuscripts of writers
from Chaucer to James Joyce. Combined with their antiques,
the townhouse museum library and garden are a treat for
anyone who appreciates first editions.

Time Needed: 45 minutes.

Tours/Programs: Special child-oriented tours available by
appointment.

Codes: 🐎 🚐 ♈

Rough and Tumble Engineer's Museum

See Lancaster, page 180.

Ryerss Museum

Burholme Park
Cottman and Central Avenues
Philadelphia, PA 19111
(215) 745-3061

Hours: Sunday 1-4 PM, group tours by appointment. Library
open Friday-Sunday 10 AM-5 PM.

Cost: Free, donation appreciated.

Description: Family treasures like a stuffed alligator mix
with collections of armor, footwear and clothes from around
the world, children's toys, and furniture.

Codes: ♿ 🐎 🚐

Sanderson Museum

Route 100
Chadds Ford, PA 19317
(215) 388-6545, or 696-3234

Hours: Saturday and Sunday 1-4:30 PM.

Cost: Free, but donation requested.

Description: Christian Sanderson saved almost everything from his associations with the Wyeths and the Brandywine Valley. Also memorabilia from Revolutionary War, Civil War, WWI and WWII.

Driving: I-95 south to Rte. 322 west to Rte. 1 south to Chadds Ford. Turn right onto Rte. 100 north. Museum is 100 yards ahead.

Codes: 🦌 🚐

Streitweiser Foundation's Trumpet Museum

Fairway Farm, Vaughan Road
Pottstown, PA 19464
(215) 327-1351

Hours: By appointment only; get directions when you call.

Cost: Suggested donation of $2.50.

Description: 400 brass instruments as well as sheet music, prints, recordings, books and figurines—all related to trumpets.

Codes: 🚐

Toy Train Museum

See Lancaster, page 180.

University Museum of Archaeology and Anthropology

University of Pennsylvania
33rd and Spruce Streets
Philadelphia, PA 19104
(215) 898-4000, or 222-7777 for schedule of events.

Hours: Tuesday-Saturday 10 AM-4:30 PM, Sunday 1-5 PM. Closed Mondays, holidays, and summer Sundays.

Cost: $2.00 suggested donation.

Description: Museum of Archaeology/Anthropology fits in well with almost any world culture children might be studying in school. Investigate mummies and cuneiform tablets, kachina dolls and tikis. Free children's films on Saturday mornings from October-March. Pyramid Children's Shop full of unusual, inexpensive treasures for active play.

Time Needed: 1-2 hours.

Tours/Programs: Excellent school programs arranged in advance. Foreign language tours available upon request.

Eating: Cafeteria-style restaurant.

Codes: ♿ 🍴 🚐 ♫

Wagner Free Institute of Science

Montgomery Avenue and 17th Street
Philadelphia, PA 19121
(215) 763-6529

Hours: Tuesday-Friday 9:30 AM-4 PM, Sunday 12 Noon-3 PM. Closed Saturdays and holidays.

Cost: Free, $.50 per child for Discovery Room.

Description: Collections of seashells, fossils, insects, minerals, birds and mammals. Interesting nature programs scheduled daily for grade school children; Educational Loan Boxes available to teachers. Discovery Room for children 6-10 years.

Eating: Picnic table area.

Codes: 🍴 🚐

From 1790 to 1800, Philadelphia was the capital of the United States.

War Library and Museum

1805 Pine Street
Philadelphia, 19103
(215) 735-8196

Hours: Monday-Friday 10 AM-4 PM, evenings and weekends by appointment.

Cost: Free.

Description: Civil War documents and treasures, many donated by their original owners. Drummer Boy exhibit extols the importance of those patriotic young communicators.

Time Needed: 1 hour.

Tours/Programs: Personal guided tours on several levels depending upon visitor's knowledge of the period.

Codes: Steep town house stairs make the building inaccessible for wheeled vehicles of any sort.

Watch and Clock Museum of the NAWCC

See Lancaster, page 181.

Wharton Esherick Museum

Box 595
Paoli, PA 19301
(215) 644-5822

Hours: March-December, Saturday 10 AM-5 PM, Sunday 1-5.

Cost: $3.00 adults, $2.00 children under 12.

Description: Every inch of the sculptor's house and studio was handcrafted with enthusiasm and a sense of humor. Coat pegs carved to resemble friends, handcarved free-form stairs, walls, furniture, even light switches. Call for reservations.

Driving: Curator gives directions when reservation is made.

Codes: 🥾 🚌 ☂

Winterthur

See Glimpses of History, page 42.

Wistar Institute Museum

36th and Spruce Streets
Philadelphia, PA 19104
(215) 898-3708   (closed until 1990)

Woodruff Indian Museum

See Bridgeton, page 161.

ETHNIC HERITAGE MUSEUMS

Afro-American Historical and Cultural Museum

7th and Arch Streets
Philadelphia. PA 19106
(215) 574-0380

Hours: Tuesday-Saturday 10 AM-5 PM, Sunday 12 Noon-6 PM. Closed holidays.

Cost: $1.50 adults, $.75 children under 12.

Description: Look for special exhibit just for children.

Codes: ♿ ✟ 🚐 ⚶

American Swedish Historical Museum

1900 Pattison Avenue
Philadelphia, PA 19145
(215) 389-1776

Hours: Tuesday-Friday 10 AM-4 PM, Saturday 12 Noon-4 PM. Closed Sundays, Mondays and holidays.

Cost: $1.50 adults, $1.00 senior citizens and students, free for children under 12 accompanied by an adult.

Description: Galleries, special exhibits and lots of fun activities.

Codes: ✟ 🚐 ⚶

Balch Institute for Ethnic Studies

18 South 7th Street
Philadelphia, PA 19106
(215) 925-8090

Hours: Monday-Saturday 10 AM-4 PM.

Cost: Free.

Description: Good place to start to understand the immigration experience. Trace ancestry and drop marbles in the giant ethnic tally bank. Many good programs through Education Department.

Codes: ♿ ✟ 🚐 ⚶

Blockson Afro-American Collection

Temple University Libraries
Sullivan Hall, Broad Street and Berks Mall
Philadelphia, PA 19122
(215) 787-6632

Hours: Monday-Friday 9 AM-5 PM.

Cost: Free.

Description: 40,000 items dating from the 16th century. Books, paper and ephemera collected by curator Charles Blockson. John Mosley photographs from the 1940s and 1950s.

Codes:

Donegal Society

Wayne, PA 19087
(215) 687-5431

German Society of Pennsylvania

611 Spring Garden Street
Philadelphia, PA 19123
(215) 627-4365

Hours: Library: Wednesday and Thursday 11 AM-5 PM, Saturday 10 AM-4 PM.

Cost: Free.

Description: Founded in 1764, this is America's oldest German organization. Library has programs, exhibits and special events.

Codes:

Ile-Ife Museum of Afro-American Culture

2544 Germantown Avenue
Philadelphia, PA 19133
(215) 225-7565

Cost: Museum free, tour $3.00. By appointment only.

Codes:

Mennonite Heritage Center

See Lancaster, page 175.

National Museum of American Jewish History

Independence Mall East, 55 North Fifth Street
Philadelphia, PA 19106
(215) 923-3811

Hours: Monday-Thursday 10 AM-5 PM, Sunday 12 Noon-5 PM, Fridays in June, July and August, 10 AM-3 PM.

Cost: $1.75 adults, $1.50 senior citizens and students, $1.25 children under 12, under 5 free.

Description: Only museum in the country dedicated exclusively to the Jewish role in the growth and development of America.

Codes: ♿ 👕 🚐

Polish American Cultural Association

308 Walnut Street
Philadelphia, PA 19106
(215) 922-1700

Hours: Opens October 1988; call for hours.

Cost: Free.

Description: Exhibits reflect the social and cultural heritage of Americans of Polish descent.

Codes: 👕 🚐

Scottish Historic and Research Society of Delaware Valley

102 Saint Paul's Road
Ardmore, PA 19003
(215) 649-4144

Library open by reservation. School programs available.

The capital of Pennsylvania
is Harrisburg.

HISTORIC PLACES OF WORSHIP

Philadelphia's earliest charter granted religious freedom to all, and immigrants came to these shores with high hopes. The places listed here encompass only a few of many diverse forms of worship. For more information, contact the Old Philadelphia Churches Historic Association (phone number changes annually; call Christ Church for current number).

Arch Street Meeting House

See Free Quaker Meeting House, page 82.

Beth Shalom Synagogue

Old York Road and Foxcroft Road, Elkins Park, PA 19117
(215) 887-1342

Designed by Frank Lloyd Wright, one of America's greatest architects, the building is intended to represent Mount Sinai. A 30-minute tour further explains Wright's symbolism.

Bryn Athyn Swedenborgian Cathedral

Route 232 and Paper Mill Road, Bryn Athyn, PA 19009
(215) 947-0266

A Gothic shrine with intricate details crafted by dedicated artisans. Make a reservation to visit the nearby Glencairn Museum while in Bryn Athyn.

Cathedral of the Immaculate Conception

816 North Franklin Street, Philadelphia, PA 19123
(215) 922-2222

The largest Ukrainian Catholic cathedral in the world. Notice its famous golden dome.

Cathedral Basilica of Saints Peter and Paul

18th and Race Streets, Philadelphia, PA 19103
(215) 561-1313

Headquarters of the Philadelphia Archdiocese of Roman Catholic churches. Can seat 2,000 at each mass.

Christ Church

2nd and Market Streets, Philadelphia, PA 19106
(215) 922-1695

Considered the birthplace of the Protestant Episcopal Church in the United States. Seven signers of the Declaration of Independence worshipped here, each with his own pew in which he sat with his family. Look for some of their names on the pews. Ben Franklin and other colonial heroes are buried in Christ Church Burial Ground at 5th and Arch.

Ephrata Cloisters

See Lancaster, page 173.

Free Quaker Meeting House

5th and Arch Streets, Independence Mall, Philadelphia, PA 19106
(215) 923-6777 (answered by Junior League)

William Penn's Holy Experiment is reviewed in a short slide show. Exhibit has artifacts and Bibles from early Quaker life in America.

Mennonite Meeting House

6119 Germantown Avenue, Philadelphia, PA 19144
(215) 843-0943

Meeting place for the first Mennonite congregation in the colonies, all restored to look as it did in the late 1700s, including the well in the basement.

Mikveh Israel Synagogue

44 North 4th Street, Philadelphia, PA 19106
(215) 922-5446

The oldest synagogue on Philadelphia, second oldest in the country. Tour includes synagogue and adjacent National Museum of American Jewish History.

Mother Bethel A.M.E. Church

419 Richard Allen Avenue, Philadelphia, PA 19147
(215) 925-0616

First African Methodist Episcopal church. Tour explains the history of black ownership and shows the beautiful, stained-glass windows.

Old First Reformed Church

4th Street and Race Street, Philadelphia, PA 19106
(215) 922-4566

German refugees established this church in 1727. Don't miss
the nativity scene in the courtyard with live animals, last two
weeks in the December.

Old Pine Street Presbyterian Church

Fourth and Pine Streets, Philadelphia, PA 19106
(215) 925-8051

The only remaining Colonial Presbyterian church in Philadelphia. When the British occupied the city in the Revolution, it
was used as a hospital and then as a stable for the cavalry.

Old Saint Joseph's Church

Willings Alley, near 4th and Walnut Streets
Philadelphia PA 19106
(215) 923-1733

Oldest Roman Catholic Church in Philadelphia. Founded in
1732, it was the only church in the Colonies or England where
public celebration of the Mass was permitted by law.

Old Swedes Church

606 Church Street, Wilmington, DE 19801
(302) 652-5629

Oldest church in the United States—originally Lutheran, then
Protestant Episcopal. An outstanding brochure explains it all.

Our Lady of Czestochowa

Ferry Road, Doylestown, PA 18901
(215) 345-0600

This replica of a 12th-century shrine in Poland stands in a
lovely 240-acre setting. Stained glass windows are among the
largest in the world.

Saint Peter's Episcopal Church

313 Pine Street, Philadelphia, PA 19106
(215) 925-5968

A beautiful red brick church with box pews, built in 1761.
George and Martha Washington worshipped here. Graveyard
has many distinguished residents, including seven Indian
chiefs.

Nature

Animals and other living things have great appeal for children. Zoos provide animals to look at, and Farms have animals to touch. Nature Centers have animals to look *for* and an abundance of insect, bird and plant life. The key is to match a child's interest to the place you visit.

Most places in this section offer pamphlets for the curious, tours or lectures for those who want to know more, and exciting children's programs throughout the year. When a walk and beautiful surroundings are enough, visit a Garden or an Arboretum.

Look for the Natural History and Science Museums in the preceding chapter.

AQUARIUMS AND CAVES

New Jersey State Aquarium

Waterfront at Mickel Boulevard
Camden, NJ 08101

Description: OPENS 1990. Under the auspices of The Philadelphia Zoo, the aquarium center focuses on the waters of New Jersey and the North Atlantic. A 600,000-gallon ocean tank contains large sharks. Outdoor naturalistic exhibits let visitors view the wildlife of the Pine Barrens and upland ponds and streams. Kids will delight in lab activities and the different demonstrations presented daily.

Crystal Cave

RD 3
Kutztown, PA 19530
(215) 683-6765

Hours: March-April, daily 9 AM-5 PM; May, Monday-Friday 9 AM-5 PM, Saturday Sunday and holidays 9 AM-6 PM; Memorial Day-Labor Day, Monday-Friday 9 AM-6 PM, Saturday-Sunday 9 AM-7 PM; Labor Day-October 31, Monday-Friday 9 AM-5 PM, Saturday-Sunday 9 AM-6 PM; November, Saturday-Sunday 9 AM-5 PM.

Cost: $4.50 adults, $2.25 children 6-12.

Description: Visit the cave and its underground formations, then go outside and enjoy 125 acres of nature trails, picnic area, Indian tepees, playground, and various shops.

Time Needed: 1 to 2 hours.

Tours/Programs: Must go on tour through cave, approximately 45 minutes including slide show at the beginning.

Eating: Picnic area. Fast food and local specialties available during peak season.

Driving: PA Turnpike west to Morgantown Exit 22. Follow I-176 north to Rte. 422 west to Rte. 222 north towards Allentown. Follow signs to Kutztown, then signs for Crystal Cave (very well marked).

Codes: 🧍 🚐

FARMS

Amish Farm; Homestead; Village

See Lancaster, pages 170 and 171.

Colonial Pennsylvania Plantation

See Villages and Homesteads, page 46.

Howell Living History Farm

Box 187, R.R. 2, Hunter Road
Titusville, NJ 08560
(609) 737-3299, or 397-0449

Hours: January-March, Saturday 10 AM-3 PM; April-May, Tuesday-Friday 10 AM-1 PM, Saturday 10 AM-4 PM, Sunday Noon-4 PM; June-July, Wednesday-Friday 10 AM-1 PM, Saturday 10 AM-4 PM, Sunday 12 Noon-4 PM; August, Saturday 4 PM-9 PM, hayrides 5-8 PM; September-November, Tuesday-Friday 10 AM-1 PM, Saturday 10 AM-4 PM, Sunday 12 Noon-4 PM. Group tours by appointment.

Cost: Free, donations appreciated.

Description: Join the farming life. Help plant, pick or grind corn. Care for animals and crops with 19th-century implements. Make soap or ice cream.

Time Needed: 1 hour.

Tours/Programs: Living History Programs open to the public offer year 'round activities of life as it was in the early 1900s. Call ahead or see Calendar of Events and time your visit to coincide with craft days or organized activities.

Eating: Picnic area.

Driving: I-95 north into New Jersey. Take first NJ exit, follow Rte. 29 north for 8 miles toward Lambertville. Right on Valley Road for 1½ miles, entrance on left.

Codes: ♿ 🚌

The capital of New Jersey is Trenton.

Merrymead Farm

2222 Valley Forge Road (Route 363)
Lansdale, PA 19446
(215) 584-4410

Hours: Summer months, Monday-Saturday 9 AM-10 PM,
Sunday 12 Noon-10 PM; winter months, Monday-Saturday
9 AM-8 PM, Sunday 12 Noon-8 PM.

Cost: Free.

Description: Busy, family-owned and -operated farm with
constant supply of new baby animals being born. Touch the
sheep, donkey, goat, cows and calves. Sheepshearing in spring,
live nativity in winter. Cows milked 3:30-6 PM.

Time Needed: 1 hour.

Eating: Picnic tables. Assorted foods available including deli-
cious homemade ice cream served in a pretzel cone.

Driving: I-76 (Schuylkill Expressway) west to Rte. 202 south,
to Rte. 422 north, to Rte. 363 north (Valley Forge Road). Continue for about 10 miles, cross Skippack Pike (Rte. 73). Farm
on right.

Codes: ♿ 🚐 ⛽

Quarry Valley Farm

Street Road
Lahaska, PA 18931
(215) 794-5882

Hours: April-December, daily 10 AM-5 PM.

Cost: $3.50 adults, $3.00 children under 12.

Description: Clean, friendly, working farm with chickens,
goats, pigs, turkeys, geese, sheep, cows and horses. Pony rides,
hay loft to play in, petting zoo, feed the animals. See the farm
equipment. Special events four times a year; birthday parties
any time.

Time Needed: 1 hour.

Eating: Snacks available, picnic under trees.

Driving: PA Turnpike to Exit 27. Follow Rte. 611 north to
Rte. 202. Follow Rte. 202 east toward New Hope. At light, with
Peddlar's Village on left, turn right onto Street Road. Farm is
½ mile ahead on the right.

Codes: ♿ 🚐 ⛽

Springton Manor Farm

Springton Road, Box 117
Glenmore, PA 19343
(215) 942-2450

Hours: Call for hours and cost.

Description: This 400-acre working farm dates back to
William Penn. Crops, sheep, pigs, chickens and more around
the barn. Watch for special paved path for wheelchairs, wandering through meadow and woods, then out to dock built for
wheelchair fishing only.

Driving: PA Turnpike west to Rte. 100 south to Rte. 30 west
to Rte. 322 north, five miles west of Downingtown. Follow Rte.
322 north through Guthriesville to Little Washington. Go
right onto Springton Road. Farm is 2½ miles ahead.

Codes: ♿ 🚐

Upper Schuylkill Valley Farm Park

Route 113
Royersford, PA 19468
(215) 948-5170

Hours: Daily 8 AM-dusk.

Cost: Free.

Description: Very good, small, county-operated farm located
on 125 acres. Great exhibit on local wildlife including black
bear, fox, quail, ferret and partridge.

Eating: Picnic area by river.

Driving: I-76 (Schuylkill Expressway) west to Rte. 202 south
to Rte. 422 west. Take Rte. 422 west from King of Prussia to
Oaks Exit. Go left under Rte. 422, take first right onto Black
Rock Road. Follow Black Rock Road approximately 4 miles. Go
left onto Rte. 113. Farm with small sign is on left immediately
after Montgomery County Geriatric and Rehabilitation
Center.

Codes: ♿ 🚐

Wentz Farmstead

See Villages and Homesteads, page 50.

GARDENS AND ARBORETUMS

Awbury Arboretum

See Germantown, page 162.

Bartram's House and Gardens

54th Street and Lindbergh Boulevard
Philadelphia, PA 19143
(215) 729-5281

Hours: Garden and grounds: daily, dawn to dusk.
House: May-October, Tuesday-Friday 10:30 AM-3:30 PM,
Saturday-Sunday 12 Noon-3:30 PM; November-April, Tuesday-
Friday 10:30 AM-3:30 PM. Closed major holidays.

Cost: Garden and grounds, free; house, $2.00 adults, $1.00
children 6-18, under 6 free.

Description: The Bartrams (father and two sons) collected
New World seeds as early as 1730, from as far away as Canada
and Florida. They planted them here, then distributed seeds
and plants to others. House tour includes description of work
and play in colonial times. Gardens are full of pungent herbs;
path along river is great for exploring.

Tours/Programs: House can be seen by tour only. Guide
often adjusts talk to appeal to children if present.

Codes: 🚐 🧎

The word Philadelphia, derived
from the Greek, means "City of
Brotherly Love."

Bowman's Hill Wildflower Preserve

Route 32, Washington Crossing State Park
Washington Crossing, PA 18977-0103
(215) 493-4076, or 862-2924

Hours: Park grounds: 9 AM-dusk. Park buildings: Monday-Saturday 9 AM-5 PM, Sunday 12 Noon-5 PM. Bowman's Hill and Tower: April-November, Monday-Friday 10 AM-5 PM, Saturday-Sunday 10 AM-6 PM. Gristmill: Daily May-October.

Cost: Hill, free; Tower, $2.00 adults, $.50 children, under 2 free, $1.50 senior citizens.

Description: 110-foot-tall Tower commands exciting 14 mile view of wildflower trails and the Delaware River Valley. Trails wind through 100 acres of beautiful nature preserve. Indoor exhibits include birds, nests, and eggs. Children are welcomed for nature movies on Sunday afternoons in winter. Watch re-enactment of Washington crossing the Delaware on Christmas Day.

Driving: Take I-95 north to New Hope/Yardley Exit; go left off the ramp onto Taylorsville Road toward New Hope. Go 3 miles to a light, go right onto Rte. 532, then left onto Rte. 32 (River Road). Visitors Center is on your right.

Codes: 🚐 ♨

Hershey Gardens

See Hershey, page 168.

Horticulture Center

See Fairmount Park, page 22.

The state bird of Delaware
is the Blue Hen chicken.

Jenkins Arboretum

631 Berwyn-Baptist Road
Devon, PA 19333
(215) 647-8870

Hours: Dawn to dusk, seven days a week.

Cost: Free.

Description: Located on a hillside, where children love to run up and down steep paths leading to the pond full of ducks and geese. Good anytime for short outing in the woods.

Driving: I-76 (Schuylkill Expressway) west to Rte. 202 south to Devon Exit. Turn left onto Devon State Road and follow it up the hill. Watch for sign about 1 mile ahead on right.

Longwood Gardens

Route 1, Box 501
Kennett Square, PA 19348-0501
(215) 388-6741

Hours: November through March, daily 9 AM-5 PM. April-October, daily 9 AM-6 PM. Indoors, daily 10 AM-5 PM.

Cost: $6.00 adults, $1.00 children 6-14, under 5 free.

Description: Giant real banana trees, massive water lily pads capable of holding a person, plants trained as topiary animals are just a few of the many horticultural wonders that appeal to children. Elaborate Christmas displays sparkle with imagination. Children's Garden introduces youngsters to the wonders of bright flowers and plants grown as mazes and tunnels; also lets them play with small fountains without getting too wet. Don't delay; Children's Garden will be dismantled in 1990.

Time Needed: 2-3 hours.

Tours/Programs: Diverse summer programs, including magic shows, "Ice Cream Concerts," and the spectacular fireworks-music-fountain symphonies are all special treats. Request schedules and reservations early. Popular activities fill up quickly, especially fireworks.

Eating: Full service restaurant, cafeteria, picnic area.

Driving: I-95 south to Rte. 322 west to Rte. 1 south. In about 8 miles, watch for signs for Longwood Gardens, located approximately 4 miles south of Chadds Ford.

Codes: ♿ ⛲ 🚐 ♿

Morris Arboretum of the University of Pennsylvania

9414 Meadowbrook Avenue
Philadelphia, PA 19118
(215) 247-5777, or 242-3399

Hours: Daily 10 AM-4 PM, open till dusk in the summer.

Cost: $2.00 adults, $1.00 senior citizens and children 6 and over, under 6 free. $.50 students in school groups.

Description: Living museum of plants. Weeping beech tree is the favorite of children who want to hide from their friends. Wide variety of plants in the rose garden, azalea meadow, fern house and other specialized growing areas. Highly recommended programs for children on weekends (call for their calendar of events) and for school groups (*see below*).

Time Needed: 1 hour.

Tours/Programs: Age-appropriate games for school groups cover the subjects of Fall Color, Plant Exploring, Importance of Bark, and many more. Tours can be adjusted for children.

Driving: I-76 (Schuylkill Expressway) west, exit at Belmont Avenue. Turn right across bridge into Manayunk, left on Main Street, right on Leverington Avenue. At dead end, turn left on Henry Avenue. Shortly after Henry runs into Ridge Avenue, turn right on Bells Mill Road, then left on Germantown Avenue and right onto Hillcrest. Hillcrest entrance on left.

Codes: ♿ 🚐 🧍

There are 4500 rivers and streams in Pennsylvania, and over 300 lakes.

Pennsylvania Horticultural Society

325 Walnut Street
Philadelphia, PA 19106
(215) 625-8250

Hours: Building: Monday-Friday 9 AM-5 PM. Garden: daily
9 AM-5 PM.

Cost: Free.

Description: Lovely 18th-century style garden, part of Independence National Historical Park. Indoor exhibits vary in child appeal. Small gift/book shop in lobby. Annual Flower Show (first week in March at the Civic Center) is guaranteed to brighten the day for all family members. Harvest Show in September at Horticulture Center has lots of activities for youngsters and competitive classes just for children.

Codes: ♀

Pennsylvania Hospital Physic Garden

8th and Pine Street
Philadelphia, PA 19107
(215) 829-3971

Hours: Dawn to dusk.

Cost: Free.

Description: A special city retreat. Ben Franklin's hospital staff requested a physic garden where they could grow medicinal herbs. This garden was restored for the Bicentennial, using the original plans. Pennsylvania Hospital's public relations office offers a good brochure describing the plants and their uses. Easy lesson for children on the vital link between plants and humans. The shaded "woodland" walk is cooling on a hot summer day.

Time Needed: ½ hour.

Codes: ♿

Pennsbury Manor

See Glimpses of History, page 37.

George Read II House and Garden

See Glimpses of History, page 29.

Scott Arboretum of Swarthmore College

Swarthmore College Campus
Swarthmore, PA 19081
(215) 328-8025

Hours: Dawn to dusk, seven days a week, all year.

Cost: Free.

Description: A miniature Stonehenge in the meadow along Crum Creek delights youngsters familiar with the English original. Tours include greenhouses and an allée of stately swamp white oaks, some 100 years old. Over 5,000 different kinds of plants are growing on the grounds.

Eating: Snack bar in Clothier Hall, open during school year.

Driving: I-76 (Schuylkill Expressway) west to Rte. 320. Follow 320 south 14.5 miles to College Avenue. Turn right on College Avenue and go one block to Arboretum office.

Codes: ♿ 🚐 🧍

Tyler Arboretum

515 Painter Road, P.O. Box 216
Lima, PA 19037
(215) 566-5431

Hours: Dawn to dusk, seven days a week, all year.
Bookstore: April-October, daily 12 Noon-4 PM.

Cost: $3.00 adults, $1.00 children, under 6 free.

Description: More than 700 acres adjoin the 2600 acres of
Ridley Creek State Park, so visitors get a true feeling of the
natural countryside. Well-marked trails appeal to energetic
children any time of year. Pets allowed if on leashes. Labeled
trees provide educational opportunities. October Pumpkin
Day has everything from free pumpkins to a haunted barn.

Tours/Programs: Natural craft and nature programs for
ages 4 and over. Summer day camps.

Eating: No food allowed. Snacks available in bookstore.

Driving: From Philadelphia, take I-95 south to 452 north.
Left on Painter Road, entrance on the right.

Codes: 🚐 ♿

Winterthur

See Glimpses of History, page 42.

The state flower of
Pennsylvania is
the mountain laurel.

NATURE CENTERS

Airdrie Forest Preserve

Fennerton Road
Paoli, PA 19301
(215) 647-5380 (answers Toland's Open Land Conservancy)

Hours: Daylight hours.

Cost: Free.

Description: 75 woodland acres offer opportunities for walks in the woods and nature appreciation. Trails do not cover the whole preserve but are just the right length for children.

Driving: From Philadelphia, follow Rte. 30 west to Paoli. At center of Paoli, immediately after the Paoli train station, go right on North Valley Road, then right on Central Avenue, then left on Fennerton. Watch carefully for small sign on right.

Codes: 🚐

Andorra Natural Area

See Fairmount Park, page 22.

Ashland Nature Center of the Delaware Nature Education Society

Brackenville Rd. near Ashland Covered Bridge, P.O. Box 700
Hockessin, DE 19707
(302) 239-2334

Hours: Monday-Friday 8:30 AM-4:30 PM, Saturday 9 AM-3 PM. Closed Sunday and holidays.

Cost: Non-members subject to fee for trail use.

Description: Indoor Discovery Room has puppets, nature books, rocks, an Indian Hut and more. Walk the trails with a brochure and keep an eye open for the excellent trail descriptions. Comprehensive summer programs for children.

Eating: Picnic tables.

Driving: I-95 south to Delaware Avenue Exit (Rte. 52 north). Follow Rte. 52 north through Greenville, then go left onto 82 north. After 4 miles, Rte. 82 takes a sharp left. After the railroad tracks, go left on an unmarked road, go through the covered bridge, and watch for Nature Center on right.

Codes: ♿ 🚐 🦅

Briar Bush Nature Center

Edge Hill Road
Abington, PA 19001
(215) 887-6603

Hours: Trails: open until dusk. Pond, Observatory, Museum: Monday-Saturday 9 AM-5 PM, Sunday 1-5 PM.

Cost: Free. Discovery Den, $1.00 per child.

Description: Twelve acres with paths that wind around ponds and well-marked bird observatory. Inside, Discovery Den for preschoolers and lots of hands-on material for all ages: hold a mouse skull next to a cow's skull, feel different animal "coverings."

Tours/Programs: Many good programs, including summer day camps and trips to Baltimore Aquarium. Advance reservations required.

Eating: Benches and picnic tables outside.

Driving: PA Turnpike to Willow Grove Exit. At end of exit ramp, turn left onto Rte. 611 south, go about 3 miles, and turn right on Edge Hill Road. Briar Bush is ½ mile on right.

Codes: ♿ ✈ 🚐 ♀

Camden County Environmental Studies Center

Park Drive and Estaugh Avenue
Berlin, NJ 08009
(609) 768-1598

Hours: Daily 8:30 AM-4 PM.

Cost: Free.

Description: Small nature center with five miles of walking trails. Emphasis on group programs. Outstanding reference materials.

Eating: Picnic areas in park.

Driving: Ben Franklin Bridge to New Jersey, follow Rte. 30 for approximately 15 miles into Berlin. In the middle of the business district, go right onto Broad Avenue and continue to the end. Entrance is straight ahead.

Codes: ♿ ✈ 🚐

Churchville Nature Center

501 Churchville Lane
Churchville, PA 18966
(215) 357-4005

Hours: Wednesday-Saturday 10 AM-5 PM, Tuesday and Sunday 12 Noon-5 PM. Closed Mondays and holidays.

Cost: Free.

Description: Trail map available in nature center to direct you along fun trails winding around beehives, ponds, quarry pits, reservoir and marsh. Outdoor classrooms revel in the wonders of nature. Lots of ducks and other wildlife. *See also* page 133.

Eating: Picnic tables.

Driving: PA Turnpike to Willow Grove Exit 27 (Rte. 611). Follow Rte. 611 north to Street Road (Rte. 132). Turn right on Rte. 132 east, then left on Rte. 232 north. At first light, turn right onto Bristol Road. At first light, turn left onto Churchville Lane. Cross lake, Nature Center on left.

Codes: ♿

Cool Valley Preserve

Cool Valley Road
Paoli, PA 19301
(215) 647-5380 (answers Toland's Open Land Conservancy)

Hours: Daylight hours.

Cost: Free.

Description: Peaceful outing with walk along nature trails.

Driving: From Philadelphia, go west on Rte. 30 to Paoli. At the center of Paoli, immediately after train station, go right on North Valley Road, left on Swedesford, then right on Shadow Oak Drive. Turn right on Cool Valley Road; Entrance is on your right. Watch carefully for sign.

Codes: 🚐

The state tree of Pennsylvania is the hemlock.

Four Mills Nature Reserve

Wissahickon Valley Watershed
12 Morris Road
Ambler, PA 19002
(215) 646-8866

Hours: Monday-Friday 10 AM-5 PM, Saturday 10 AM-2:30 PM. Closed Sunday.

Cost: Free.

Description: Good small nature center in old barn with many fun activities, like matching animals with their tracks and comparing the sizes of birds nests. Learn about food chains and how birds' beaks adapt to the type of food they eat.

Programs: Many throughout the year, including brief summer camps for toddlers and preschoolers.

Driving: PA Turnpike to Exit 26. Go straight after toll booths onto Pennsylvania Avenue. Go right to dead end, take left onto Bethlehem Pike (Rte. 309). Just after train station and small bridge, take a right at restaurant onto Morris Road. Nature Center is one mile ahead on the right.

Codes: ♿ ⛺ 🚐 🐾

Hawk Mountain Sanctuary

Route 2
Kempton, PA 19529
(215) 756-6961

Hours: Daily 8 AM-5 PM.

Cost: Visitor's Center free; hiking trails $2.50 adults, $1.00 children 6-12.

Description: Spectacular bird watching, especially during migration. Sanctuary dedicated to conservation of birds of prey. Stop at the Visitor's Center to get their excellent brochure describing the 2,200 acre refuge and its inhabitants. Trail lookout sites offer fine photo opportunities.

Eating: Picnics permitted at lookout sites.

Driving: PA Turnpike to the Northeast Extension to Exit 33. Go west on Rte. 22, north on Rte. 61, north on Rte. 895, and east on Rte. 737. Sanctuary is 6 miles short of Kempton.

Codes: 🚐 🐾

George Lorimer Nature Preserve

North Valley Road
Paoli, PA 19301
(215) 647-5380 (answers Toland's Open Land Conservancy)

Hours: Daylight.

Cost: Free.

Description: Trails for nature walks any time of year.

Driving: From Philadelphia follow Rte. 30 west to Paoli. In the center of Paoli, immediately after Paoli train station, go right on North Valley Road, then right on Swedesford Road, then left onto North Valley again. Entrance is on the right. Watch carefully for sign.

Codes: 🚗

Mill Grove, Audubon Wildlife Sanctuary

P.O. Box 473
Audubon, PA 19407
(215) 666-5593

Hours: Grounds: daily, 7 AM-dusk. Museum: Tuesday-Saturday 10 AM-4 PM, Sunday 1-4 PM. Closed Mondays, Thanksgiving, Christmas, New Year's.

Cost: Free.

Description: First (and only remaining) American home of artist/ naturalist John James Audubon. Giant murals on the mansion's walls depict Audubon's adventures and many bird scenes. Restored studio and taxidermy room. Well-marked trails are short enough for young children to complete. Take along crayons and paper and let young artists imitate Audubon.

Programs: Folder available listing 174 species of birds sighted.

Eating: No eating allowed. Picnic area at adjacent Perkiomen Valley Park.

Driving: I-76 (Schuylkill Expressway) west to Rte. 202 south to Rte. 422 west to Audubon Exit (Rte. 363). Bear right along exit ramp, then left onto Audubon Road. Mill Grove is straight ahead at dead end.

Codes: 👫

Nature Center of Charlestown

P.O. Box 82, Route 29 and Hollow Road
Devault, PA 19432
(215) 935-9777

Hours: Monday-Saturday 9 AM-5 PM, Sunday 12 Noon-5 PM.

Cost: Free.

Description: Low key, friendly Center features the snakes and toads of everyday life. Play with them inside, then go out and find where they live in the wild. Discover land and water natural habitats, from beehives to crayfish pools in the stream, with knowledgeable enthusiastic guides.

Tours/Programs: Fun exploratory summer programs for youngsters and their families. Children grades 7-12 can volunteer to be summer nature camp aides for the junior group.

Eating: No picnics or eating allowed.

Driving: I-76 (Schuylkill Expressway) west to Rte. 202 south. Take Rte. 29 exit, go right (29 north) to Hollow Road. Turn left on Hollow Road, watch for small parking lot on right. Park there, then walk over bridge and up hill to Nature Center and buildings.

Codes: 🚐 👫

Nolde Forest Evironmental Education Center

RD 1, Box 392
Reading, PA 19607
(215) 775-1411

Hours: Outdoors: dawn to dusk.
Office and mansion: Monday-Friday 8 AM-4 PM.

Cost: Free.

Description: Truly for nature appreciation. Hiking OK but no swimming, eating, or camping. Stop by the office and pick up a topographical leaflet, then enjoy 600 acres of protected land. A few paved trails for wheelchairs and strollers.

Tours/Programs: Good school group programs. Call ahead.

Driving: PA turnpike to Morgantown Exit 22. Take Morgantown Road onto Rte. 625 for two miles, entrance is after 2nd sign saying Nolde Forest. Watch carefully, entrance is obscure.

Codes: 🚐

PAWS Wildlife Sanctuary

(Preservation and Wildlife Society)
Hainesport-Mount Laurel Road
Mount Laurel, NJ 08054
(609) 778-8795

Hours: Wednesday-Sunday 10 AM-4 PM.

Cost: $1.00 per person.

Description: Plenty for all ages to see and learn while they play. Observe a screech owl from the edge of its cage, climb through a "burrow." Outside adventures offer unusual animals such as miniature horses, arctic fox, miniature pigs, and regular deer, skunk, turkey, raccoon. Pet sheep, goat, ferret, and snake. Don't miss the barn. Nature films Saturday afternoons in January and February.

Tours/Programs: Outstanding programs for all ages, including "pet therapy" outreach: visiting hospital pediatric wards, handicap centers, nursing and convalescent homes.

Eating: Picnic tables.

Driving: From Philadelphia, cross Delaware River on Ben Franklin or Walt Whitman Bridge and pick up I-295 north to Mount Holly. Take Rte. 38 north to first light, go right onto Hartford Road to first stop sign. Left on Hainesport Road, and go ½ mile. Park in lot and walk down dirt drive.

Codes: ♿ ✈ 🚕 ⚔

Peace Valley Nature Center

170 Chapman Road, RD 1
Doylestown, PA 18901
(215) 345-7860

Hours: Tuesday-Sunday 10 AM-4 PM.

Cost: Free.

Description: Beautiful grounds, very good education programs. Nature Center has a working solar addition. *See also* page 134.

Eating: Snack bar and picnic areas.

Driving: PA Turnpike to Willow Grove Exit 27. Follow Rte. 611 north into Doylestown. Turn left onto Rte. 313 west, go for approximately 2 miles and turn left onto New Galena Road, then left again onto Chapman Road.

Codes: ⚔

Pennypack Environmental Center

8600 Verree Street
Philadelphia, PA 19115
(215) 671-0440

Hours: Dawn to dusk.

Cost: Free.

Description: More than 1200 acres of native plant and small animal wildlife within the rapidly growing city. Small indoor center has aquarium, touch room, and natural history exhibits. Many good programs for children in school groups and on weekends and summer. *See also* page 141.

Eating: picnic tables.

Codes: 🚐 ♿

Pool Wildlife Sanctuary

601 Orchid Place
Emmaus, PA 18049
(215) 965-4397

Hours: Monday-Friday 9 AM-3 PM.

Cost: $.50 donation requested.

Description: Good trail guides lead visitors through shady and sunny habitats in the sanctuary. Environmental Education Center has rocks and minerals, tree and nest exhibit, and more.

Tours/Programs: Family programs; trout roast in May.

Eating: Picnic tables.

Driving: PA Turnpike to Northeast extension. At Exit 33 go east on Rte. 22, then south on Rte. 309, getting off at Cedar Crest Boulevard Exit. Go right at the exit onto Cedar Crest Boulevard. Go two miles then, take a left on Riverbend Road, right on Orchid Place. Watch for old stone barn with red door and the sanctuary on your right.

Codes: ♿ 🐴

The state flower of New Jersey is the purple violet.

Rancocas Nature Center

Rancocas Road, RD 1
Mount Holly, NJ 08060
(609) 261-2495

Hours: Tuesday-Sunday 9 AM-5 PM, Monday trails open,
Nature Center closed.

Cost: Free.

Description: Part of New Jersey Audubon Society park system. Small nature center with exhibits and hands-on material. Short, very well-marked outdoor trail with interesting, instructive trail guide. Longer trails wind through Lenape Indian Reservation.

Tours/Programs: New Jersey Audubon system programs.

Driving: From Philadelphia, cross Delaware River to New Jersey, take Rte. I-295 north across Rancocas Creek. Take Exit 45A (Willingboro/Mount Holly) and follow Rancocas Road for 1.7 miles. Nature Center is on your right.

Codes: 🚐 🦽

Riverbend Environmental Education Center

Box 2, Springmill Road
Gladwyne, PA 19035
(215) 527-5234

Hours: 8:30 AM to dusk.

Cost: Free.

Description: 26 acres of land, stone farm house, working water wheel/springhouse and barn. Trails to stimulate curiosity and enthusiasm for the environment.

Tours/Programs: Many programs and special events for children, school groups, and for teachers. Call for newsletter and schedule of events. Fun Saturday and summer programs. Barn available for birthday parties.

Driving: I-76 (Schuylkill Expressway) west to Conshohocken exit. Go right at the light onto Front Street. Follow signs for Rte. 23 (Conshohocken State Road). Go left on Spring Mill Road, pass Philadelphia Country Club. Nature Center parking lot is at the end of Spring Mill.

Codes: 🚐 🏭

Schuylkill Valley Nature Center

Hagy's Mill Road
Philadelphia, PA 19128
(215) 482-7300

Hours: Monday-Saturday 8:30 AM-5 PM, Sunday 12 Noon-5 PM.

Cost: $3.00 adults, $2.00 children.

Description: Within the city limits, SVNC boasts 500 acres of nature trails, streams, ponds, forests and wildlife habitats. Large Education Building has spacious young child's Discovery Room with multitude of fun activities, outstanding bookstore/gift shop and a wide variety of quality programs for all ages.

Tours/Programs: Family programs offered every weekend. Special holiday programs blend natural crafts with seasonal themes.

Eating: Picnic area.

Driving: I-76 (Schuylkill Expressway) west to Belmont Avenue Exit. Cross bridge into Manayunk and go straight up the hill on Greene Lane. At the top, take a left onto Ridge Avenue. Go 2 miles, turn left onto Port Royal Avenue, then right onto Hagy's Mill Road. Nature center is on the left.

Codes: ♿ � ⛟ 🐦

Silver Lake Nature Center

1006 Bath Road
Bristol, PA 19007
(215) 785-1177

Hours: Tuesday-Saturday 10 AM-5 PM, Sunday 12 Noon-5 PM.

Cost: Free.

Description: Part of the Bucks County Park system, Silver Lake has two miles of trails. Bird Observation in converted garage. Please Touch Table and variety of frogs, turtles, and fish. *See also* page 135.

Eating: Picnic tables.

Driving: PA Turnpike to Delaware Valley Exit 27. Take Rte. 13 south to 2nd light. Turn right on Bath Road. Pass Lower Bucks Hospital. Nature Center on right.

Codes: ⛟

Tinicum National Environmental Center

86th Street and Lindbergh Boulevard
Philadelphia, PA 19153
(215) 365-3118

Hours: Outdoors: daily 8 AM-sunset. Visitor's Center: 8-4:30.

Cost: Free.

Description: Largest tidal wetland in Pennsylvania. Trails
are open all year for walking and good bird watching: over 280
species of birds have been sighted here. Programs are adult-
oriented or for older children.

Eating: Picnics allowed along trails.

Codes: &.

PLANETARIUMS

Eastern College Planetarium

Saint Davids, PA 19085
(215) 341-0800

Description: Special holiday show about Star of David. Call.

Fels Planetarium

See Franklin Institute, page 61.

New Jersey State Museum and Planetarium

See New Jersey State Museum, page 66.

North Museum Planetarium

See North Museum, page 177.

Reading Public Museum Planetarium

See Reading Public Museum, page 73 (school groups only).

Rittenhouse Lab Observatory

209 South 33rd Street
Philadelphia, PA 19104-6394
(215) 898-8176

Hours: Fall-Winter, Monday and Thursday evenings 7:30-9;
Spring-Summer, Monday and Thursday evenings 9-10:30 PM.

Cost: Free.

Description: Roof telescopes and instructor to help visitors.

Codes: 🚐

ZOOS

Brandywine Zoo

1001 North Park Drive
Wilmington, DE 19802
(302) 571-7788

Hours: Daily 10 AM-4 PM. Exotic Animal House: April-
October, daily 11 AM-3:45 PM; November-March, open by
appointment.

Cost: April-October, $2.00 adults, $.75 children 3-15, under 3
free; November-March, everyone free.

Description: Small, compact and clean. Good variety of
animals in well-planned naturalistic habitats built on the side
of a hill. Otter exhibit is especially fun. Located in Brandywine
Park.

Time Needed: 1 hour.

Tours/Programs: Tours available upon request; special programs throughout the year. "Adopt-an-animal" opportunities.

Eating: Snack bar, picnic area.

Driving: I-95 south towards Wilmington. Exit at Concord
Pike (Rte. 202). Follow 202 south to 2nd light, bear right onto
Baynard Boulevard. Take Baynard to 18th Street, right on
18th, right at first stop sign. Left at sign for Zoo. Park on the
street.

Codes: ♿ 🚐 👶

Cohanzick Zoo

See Bridgeton, page 159.

The state bird of
New Jersey is the
American goldfinch.

Elmwood Park Zoo

Harding Boulevard
Norristown, PA 19401
(215) 277-DUCK   or (215) 272-8080 (Borough Hall)

Hours: Daily 10 AM-4:30 PM. Closed Thanksgiving, Christmas, New Year's. Children's Zoo closed in winter.

Cost: Free.

Description: Small and easily manageable for young children, who love to view the zoo from the elevated boardwalk. U.S. History exhibit (Zoo America) features the Wild West's bison, elk, and prairie dog village. Small petting zoo.

Time Needed: 1 hour.

Tours/Programs: Workshops available for groups and sporadically on summer weekends. Special programs in small amphitheater.

Eating: Snack bar and picnic tables.

Driving: I-76 (Schuylkill Expressway) west to Rte. 202 north, past the Court at King of Prussia. Do not take Bridgeport exit off Rte. 202. Continue straight after the exit to 5th light. Left at this light, then first left onto Chain Street, which turns into Harding Boulevard. Watch for Zoo on right.

Codes: ♿ 🚐 ⛲ 🪑

The word Pennsylvania comes from
the Greek and means "Penn's Woods."
The state was named in honor of
William Penn's *father*.

Philadelphia Zoo

(The Philadelphia Zoological Garden)
34th Street and Girard Avenue
Philadelphia, PA 19104
(215) 243-1100

Hours: Daily 9:30 AM-5 PM. Closed Thanksgiving, December 24, 25, 31, New Year's Day.

Cost: $4.50 age 12 and over, $3.50 children 3-11, under 3 free. Extra fee for some exhibits.

Description: America's first Zoo! Always something exciting going on. Treehouse with magical entry rings offers hours of fun; Children's Zoo gives kids a chance to feed the animals. World of primates and underwater polar bear exhibit are among the many natural habitats visitors can explore from all angles.

Time Needed: 2 hours . . . up to a fun, full day.

Tours/Programs: Group tours available through Docent Office. Highly recommended workshops and special events throughout the year.

Eating: Family-style cafeteria with indoor and outdoor tables. Snack bars and picnic areas throughout the zoo.

Driving: I-76 (Schuylkill Expressway) west to Girard Avenue exit and follow signs to the ZOO. Parking available on 34th Street or Girard Avenue.

Codes: 🚶 🌲 🚌 🐾 ✂

Zoo America

See Hershey, page 169.

Performing Arts

Every child loves the magic of a stage performance, no matter which side of the lights he or she is on. The performing groups listed here put on programs specifically for children. Most groups have matinee performances, and with the exception of the glorious *Nutcracker*, most tickets are inexpensive.

The Annenberg Center's giant annual children's festival in late May offers a mind-boggling array of international talent—singing, dancing, miming and performing magnificently just for children. The Annenberg Center is at 3680 Walnut Street, Philadelphia, PA 19104; call (215) 898-6791 for information and reservations.

DANCE

Ballet des Jeunes

1447 Manoa Road
Philadelphia, PA 19151
(215) 473-2253

A troupe of thirty youngsters age 10 to 18 performs in various locations around Philadelphia and throughout the world.

Ile-Ife Center for the Arts and Humanities

2544 Germantown Avenue
Philadelphia, PA 19133
(215) 225-7565

Afro-American and Caribbean dance performances at the museum all year.

Pennsylvania Ballet Company

2525 Pennsylvania Avenue
Philadelphia, PA 19130
(215) 978-1429

Dances the classic *Nutcracker* at the Academy of Music during the holiday season.

Philadelphia Civic Ballet Company

1615 Sansom Street
Philadelphia, PA 19103
(215) 564-1505

One performance just for children each season at varying locations. Special children's holiday performance at the Free Library.

Temple University's Conwell Dance Theater

Dance Department, Seltzer Hall, 3rd Floor
Temple University
Philadelphia, PA 19122
(215) 787-6177

Young People's Performance Series of approximately five matinees places emphasis on audience participation.

MUSIC

Academy Boys Choir

Academy of Music
Broad and Locust Streets
Philadelphia, PA 19103
(215) 222-2101

Part of the Performing Arts School. Forty to sixty members ages 7-15 with repertoire from classical to Broadway.

City of Philadelphia Summer Music Programs

Department of Recreation
Belmont and Parkside Avenues
Philadelphia, PA 19131
(215) 686-0151

Free outdoor neighborhood concerts. Watch local media for announcements or call for information.

Concerto Soloists' Children's Concerts

2136 Locust Street
Philadelphia, PA 19103
(215) 735-0202

Children's concerts at WHYY (6th and Arch Streets, Philadelphia) include audience participation. Each 1-hour concert highlights a prize-winning child performer.

Philadelphia Boys Choir and Chorale

225 North 32nd Street
Philadelphia, PA 19104
(215) 222-3500

About 60 boys ages 8-13 sing with extraordinary beauty at more than forty performances each year.

Philadelphia Orchestra's Children's Concerts

Academy of Music
Broad and Locust Streets
Philadelphia, PA 19103
(215) 893-1900

Short, lively performances with a quick lesson well-camouflaged and easy to digest.

Settlement Music School Recitals

416 Queen Street
Philadelphia, PA 19147
(215) 336-0400

Student recitals one Sunday each month, in each of five branches throughout the city. Watch for special performances during the year on a single subject, like jazz, etc.

LOCAL RADIO AND TV FOR CHILDREN

Radio:

"Kid's Corner" on WXPN
University of Pennsylvania
3905 Spruce Street
Philadelphia, PA 19104

Monday-Friday 7:00-8:00 PM: Live call-in show for 6 to 12-year-olds, dealing with local issues. Call line: (215) 898-8868 or 1-800-KIDS XPN
Monday-Friday 7:30-8 PM: Music to do homework by!

Television:

"Al Albert Showcase" on WPVI-TV 6
4100 City Line Avenue
Philadelphia, PA 19131
(215) 878-9700

Saturday 11:00 AM: children's talent show (auditions and tapings on Wednesday evenings, 7-10 PM).

"Double Dare"

Taped in Philadelphia. For tickets write: Double Dare, 1775 Broadway, New York, NY 10019. Same address for contestant auditions, ages 10-13.

"Kidside" on WCAU-TV 10
City Line Avenue and Monument Avenue
Philadelphia, PA 19131
(215) 668-5700

Saturday 7:00 PM, four times a year: local issues covered by kid reporters.

THEATER & THEATRICAL FUN

Plays, puppets, clowns and films for children.

Allens Lane Art Center

Allens Lane and McCallum Streets
Philadelphia, PA 19119
(215) 248-0546

American Theater Arts for Youth

1429 Walnut Street
Philadelphia, PA 19102
(215) 563-3501, 1-800-523-4540

Annenberg Center Theatre for Children

3680 Walnut Street
Philadelphia, PA 19104-6219
(215) 898-6791

Annual children's festival in late May is fantastic!

Appel Farm Arts

P.O. Box 770
Elmer, NJ 08318
(609) 358-2472

Bucks County Playhouse

70 South Main Street, P.O. Box 313
New Hope, PA 18938
(215) 862-2041

Bushfire Theater

228 South 52nd Street
Philadelphia, PA 19143
(215) 747-9230

Camarata Opera Theater

1006 Kingston Drive
Cherry Hill, NJ 08034
(609) 428-7999

Cheltenham Playhouse Children's Theatre

439 Ashbourne Road
Philadelphia, PA 19102
(215) 379-4027

Children's Musical Theatre

Valley Forge Music Fair
176 Swedesford Road
Devon, PA 19333
(215) 644-5000

Community Education Center

3500 Lancaster Avenue
Philadelphia, PA 19104
(215) 387-1911

Delaware Children's Theater

1014 Delaware Avenue
Wilmington, DE 19806
(302) 655-1014

350-seat theater with frequent performances. Call for
reservations—they sell out quickly.

Delaware County Community College

Media, PA 19063
(215) 359-5075

Drexel University Theater

3220 Chestnut Street
Philadelphia, PA 19104
(215) 895-1929

Free Library of Philadelphia

Logan Square
Philadelphia, PA 19103
(215) 686-5372

Book concerts, magicians, music, ballet and other dance
groups, films, and plays. Many interpreted in sign language.

Fulton Opera House

12 North Prince Street, P.O. Box 1865
Lancaster, PA 17603
(717) 397-7425

Glassboro Summer Theatre

Glassboro State College
Glassboro, NJ 08028
(609) 863-6392

Grand Opera House

818 Market Street Mall
Wilmington, DE 19801
(302) 658-7897

Hedgerow Theater

146 West Rose Valley Road
Rose Valley, PA 19080
(215) 565-4211

Kaleidoscope Art Center

200 West Main Street
Lansdale, PA 19446
(215) 368-5050

Keswick Theater

291 Keswick Avenue
Glenside, PA 19038
(215) 572-7650

Museum Family Theatre

Academy of Natural Sciences
19th Street and the Parkway
Philadelphia, PA 19103
(215) 299-1054

New Freedom Theater

1346 North Broad Street
Philadelphia, PA 19121
(215) 765-2793

Performing Arts Center

Stockton State College
Pomona, NJ 08240
(609) 652-9000

Philadelphia Marionette Theater

2501 Christian Street
Philadelphia, PA 19146
(215) 732-6581

Playhouse Theater

10th and Market Streets
Wilmington, DE 19801
(302) 656-4401

Plays and Players Children's Theatre

1714 Delancey Place
Philadelphia, PA 19103
(215) 735-0630

Please Touch Museum

Virginia Evans Theater
210 North 21st Street
Philadelphia, PA 19103
(215) 963-0666

Puttin' On the Ritz Children's Theatre

915 White Horse Pike
Oaklyn, NJ 08107
(609) 858-5230

Theater Center of Philadelphia

622 South 4th Street
Philadelphia, PA 19147
(215) 925-2682

University of the Arts

Broad and Pine Streets
Philadelphia, PA 19102
(215) 875-4832

Villanova University Theatre

Villanova, PA 19085
(215) 645-4760

Walt Whitman Center

2nd and Cooper Streets
Camden, NJ 08102
(609) 757-7276

War Memorial Building

West Lafayette Street
Trenton, NJ 08608
(609) 393-4866

West Chester and Barleysheaf Players

29 Whitford Road
Lionville, PA 19353
(215) 363-7075

Recreation

The recreational activities listed here are those we find appeal most to children. If we've missed your child's favorite, please send us information so we can include it in our next edition.

Sports are divided into Active Sports and Spectator Sports. The best bargain in town is Division I college sports—28 different sports to watch up close from the sidelines or in small stadiums, low cost or free tickets, and plenty of action!

AMUSEMENT PARKS

Clementon Amusement Park

144 Berlin Road
Clementon, NJ 08021
(609) 783-0263

Hours: April to mid-June, Saturday-Sunday 12 noon-10 PM;
mid-June to October, Tuesday-Sunday 12 noon-10 PM.

Cost: $8.25, under 2 free. Water slide extra.

Description: Lots of rides for all ages including the Great
Log Flume, Crazy Dazy and Haunted House, plus kiddie helicopters, baby boats, and a space-age kiddie ride. Magicians
and clowns throughout the park.

Eating: Covered pavilions for picnics; many concession
stands.

Driving: Walt Whitman Bridge to New Jersey to Rte. 42
south. Get off at Blackwood/Clementon Exit, then follow
Rte. 534 east. Entrance to park is 4 miles ahead on the right.

Codes: &.

Dorney Park and Wildwater Kingdom

3830 Dorney Park Road
Allentown, PA 18104
(215) 395-2000

Hours: April-May, weekends (call for hours); Memorial Day weekend and June, both parks, 11 AM-6 PM; July through Labor Day, Dorney Park 11 AM-10 PM; July-August 21, Wildwater Kingdom, 10 AM-8 PM; August 22 through Labor Day, Wildwater Kingdom, 10 AM-6 PM.

Cost: Age 7 and over: $16.95 Dorney Park/Wildwater Kingdom, $12.95 Dorney Park only, $12.95 Wildwater Kingdom only. Children age 3-6: $10.00 Dorney Park/Wildwater Kingdom, $7.50 Dorney Park only, $7.50 Wildwater Kingdom only.

Description: Dorney Park is a clean amusement area with two distinct sections. The flat area, where you enter, is good for strollers and has games and rides that appeal to younger children. Up the hill are the more exciting roller coaster and gravity-defying rides for older children.

Wildwater Kingdom is the place to be on a hot summer day, with giant wave pool, Auto Kid Wash, speedslides and activity pools. Lollipop Lagoon for the youngest children.

Eating: Plenty of food available everywhere. Picnic pavilions for groups can be reserved ahead of time.

Driving: PA Turnpike to Northeast Extension to Exit 33. Follow Rte. 22 east to Rte. 309 south to Hamilton Boulevard (Rte. 222). Go left off the exit ramp and follow signs for the Parks.

Codes: &

Dutch Wonderland

2249 Route 30 East
Lancaster, PA 17602
(717) 291-1888

Hours: Easter Weekend-Memorial Day, Saturday 10 AM-6 PM, Sunday 12 noon-6 PM; Memorial Day-Labor Day, Saturday 10 AM-7 PM, Sunday 11 AM-7 PM. Day after Labor Day-October, Saturday 10 AM-6 PM, Sunday 12 Noon-6 PM.

Cost: $8.05 admission and five rides, $11.55 admission and unlimited rides. Infants and small toddlers free.

Description: Perfect amusement park for younger children. Boats, cars, trains, double splash roller coaster, high dive demonstration, monorail around the park ($1 extra).

Eating: Concession stands, cafeteria, restaurant.

Driving: PA Turnpike west to 100 south to Rte. 30 west. Watch for big, castle-like structure on right 4 miles before Lancaster. See Lancaster map, page 231.

Codes: &

Hersheypark

See Hershey, page 169.

Both Princeton and Trenton have been, briefly, the country's capital city.

Sesame Place

Oxford Valley Road
Langhorne, PA 19407
(215) 757-1100 recorded, or 752-7070

Hours: Early May to mid-June, daily 10 AM-5 PM; mid-June
to July 1, daily 10 AM-8 PM; July 2 to September 4, daily 9 AM-
8 PM; September 5-9, daily 10 AM-5 PM; mid-September to
mid-October, weekends 10 AM-5 PM.

Cost: $11.95 adults, $13.95 children, $3.00 parking.

Description: Rides and attractions feature Bert, Ernie and
the gang, but activities also abound for children up to age 13.
Outdoor climbing and jumping, indoor see-yourself-on-
television broadcasts, computer games and more.
There are some exciting water games, so visitors should have
bathing suits under clothes and wear shoes that are easy to
take off and put on several times.

Eating: Picnic tables and cafeteria with healthy kid food.

Driving: Going north from Philadelphia on Rte. 1, watch for
Oxford Valley Mall. Go left at the light immediately after the
Mall. Stay in left lane and watch for signs on left.

Codes: 🦽 🚐

The state tree of
New Jersey is
the red oak.

Six Flags Great Adventure

Route 537, P.O. Box 120
Jackson, NJ 08527
(201) 928-3500

Hours: April, May, September and October, weekends 10 AM to either 6 or 8 PM; Memorial Day to Labor Day, daily 10 AM-10 PM.

Cost: $20 adults, $13.95 age 14 and under, free under 3.

Description: More than one amusement park: 350-acre Drive-thru Safari is home to 1900 animals; big amusement park has over 100 rides; Bugs Bunny Land has 25 rides.

Eating: Food available everywhere. Picnic areas near Safari entrance and bus parking lot outside main entrance.

Driving: New Jersey Turnpike to Exit 7A, east on I-95 for 12 miles to Mount Holly-Freehold Exit 16. Watch for signs.

Codes: ♿

Storybook Land

Black Horse Pike
Cardiff, NJ 08232
(609) 641-7847

Hours: Mid-March-April, Saturday and Sunday 11 AM-5 PM; May through mid-June, weekdays 10 AM-3 PM, Saturday and Sunday 11 AM-5 PM; mid-June through Labor Day, daily 10 AM-5:30 PM; Labor Day-October, Thursday and Friday 10 AM-3 PM, Saturday and Sunday 11 AM-5 PM; November and December, 2-8:30 PM (Christmas displays).

Cost: $6.50 per person.

Description: Rides for even the youngest of Mother Goose's friends—merry-go-rounds, small cars, Flying Jumbo, and a small train to ride. Fun to feed the live animals which include sheep and goats. This park with its many shade trees is unexpectedly pleasant on hot days. More than 90,000 lights brighten the area at Christmas time.

Eating: Plenty available.

Driving: From Philadelphia, cross to New Jersey and follow I-676 south to Rte. 422 south to Rte. 322 south (Black Horse Pike) to Cardiff. Watch for white castle-like structure.

Codes: ♿

Water Buggy

2343 Lincoln Highway East (Route 30)
Lancaster, PA 17602
(717) 397-4674

Hours: Memorial Day weekend to Labor Day, 10 AM-8 PM (weather permitting).

Cost: Waterslide: $5.50 for 10 rides, $9.75 all day.
Bumper Boats: $2.00 for seven minutes.
Miniature Golf: $1.50 for 19 holes.
Early Birds: $7.00 for 20 rides (be there before 10:20 AM).
Twilight: $7.00 for all you can do from 5 PM to closing.

Description: Three water slides and one for the very young. Everyone must go down slides alone. Bumper boats in separate pool; miniature golf next to parking lot. Bleachers where you can sit and watch waterslides. Arcade nearby.

Eating: Snack Bar and picnic area.

Driving: Take PA Turnpike west, then Rte. 100 south and Rte. 30 west to just past Rte. 896. Water Buggy is on right side next to Carter's Outlet. See Lancaster map, page 231.

HARVESTING

One of the outings children are eager to repeat year after year is harvesting, whether it's picking apples from dwarf trees or cutting their own evergreen tree for the holiday season. Prices fluctuate, as do hours of operation and crops available for harvesting. We recommend you call before going.

Christmas Tree Cutting

Henry Banff
  Mullica Hill, NJ 08062
  (609) 478-4243

Chesterfield Tree Farm
  Chesterfield, NJ 08620
  (609) 298-3234

Deer Valley Tree Farm
  West Chester, PA 19380
  (215) 269-2247

Fernbrook Farm Nursery
  Bordentown, NJ 08505
  (609) 298-8282

Indian Acres Tree Farm
  Medford, NJ 08055
  (609) 953-0087

Jug Hill Christmas Tree Farm
  Yardley, PA 19064
  (215) 493-9400

Kutz's Christmas Tree Farm
  Pottstown, PA 19464
  (215) 469-6270

Malickson's Tree Farm
  Phoenixville, PA 19460
  (215) 933-9140

Pine Run Tree Farm
  Fountainville, PA 18923
  (215) 493-9400

Watson Tree Farm
  Warrington, PA 18976
  (215) 343-6561

Boswell's Tree Farm
  Collegeville, PA 19426
  (215) 584-4739

Richard T. DeCou
  Moorestown, NJ 08057
  (609)234-6113

Exley's Country Lane Nursery
  Sewell, NJ 08042
  (609) 468-5949

Haines Tree Farm
  Juliustown, NJ 08042
  (609) 894-2967

Indian Walk Tree Farm
  Wrightstown, PA 18940
  (215) 598-3518

Kimber-Vu Farm
  Phoenixville, PA 19460
  (215) 935-9559

Lucca T. Farms
  Berlin, NJ 08009
  (609) 767-0189

McArdle Tree Farm
  Mechanicsville, PA 18934
  (215) 794-7655

Train Tree Plantation
  Lumberton, NJ 08048
  (609) 261-4444

Wetherill Christmas Trees
  Chester Springs, PA 19425
  (215) 469-9472

Fruitpicking (and sometimes hayrides!)

Appleville Orchards
Route 63
Telford, PA 18969
(215) 723-6516

Conte Farms
183 Flyatt Road
Tabernacle, NJ 08088
(609) 268-1010

Four Winds Farm
Route 532/Tabernacle Road
Medford, NJ 08055
(609) 268-9113

Johnson's Corner Farm
Church and Hartford Roads
Medford, NJ 08055
(609) 654-8643

Manbeck's Orchards
Schubert Road
Bethel, PA 19507
(717) 933-4541

Northbrook Orchards
Route 842 & Northbrook
Road
West Chester, PA 19380
(215) 793-1210

Paul Valley Farm Market
Easton Road
Warrington, PA 18976
(215) 343-1285

Strawberry Acres/
Overlook Orchards Inc.
Route 145
Copley, PA 18037
(215) 262-3674

Tuck-A-Lou Orchards
Routes 619 and 538
Hardingville, NJ 08243
(609) 881-0582

Barnard's Orchards
1079 Wawaset Road
Kennett Square, PA 19348
(215) 347-2151

Duncan's Farm Market
966 Valley Forge Road
Devon, PA 19333
(215) 688-2786

Highland Orchards, Inc.
1000 Thorndale Road
West Chester, PA 19380
(215) 269-3494

Linvilla Orchards
137 W. Knowlton Road
Media, PA 19063
(215) 876-7116

Nonesuch Farm
Route 263
Buckingham, PA 18912
(215) 794-5201

Nussex Farms
880 South Five Points Road
West Chester, PA 19380
(215) 696-1133

Spring Meadow Farm
Hopwood Road
Collegeville, PA 19426
(215) 489-9540

J.G. Strock
Route 73
Blue Anchor, NJ 08037
(609) 561-3063

Warner Enterprises
Route 406
Milford, DE 19963
(302) 422-9506

PARKS AND PLAYGROUNDS

Park charts apply to parks run by the state or county or state. All parks are open from dawn to dusk.

Plan ahead! Where fishing is allowed, everyone needs a license. Anyone caught fishing without the proper credentials for that state is sure to get a fine and have all fishing equipment confiscated. We know. To get a license, call (215) 686-2489 in Pennsylvania, (609) 292-2965 in New Jersey, and (302) 736-4431 in Delaware.

All parks have walking and hiking trails throughout. Dogs are allowed in most parks as long as they stay on a leash no longer than six feet.

Picnic tables are scattered throughout most parks. Places with barbecue grills or fireplaces for cooking are designated with a mark in the "Grills" column.

One of our favorites, the Smith Memorial Playgrounds and Playhouse, is in the Fairmount Park section, page 24.

DELAWARE
New Castle County
County parks: (302) 323-6415

	Playground	Pool	Lake/Pond	Fishing	Boat Rental	Bike Paths	Bridle Paths	Snack Bar	Grills	Camping	Ice Skating	Sledding	Other
Bellevue State Park 800 Carr Road Wilmington, DE 19809 (302) 571-3390 270 acres	✦		✦	✦		✦	✦	✦			✦		Tennis.
Brandywine Creek State Park Adams Dam Road Rockland, DE 19732 (302) 571-3534 784 acres			✦	✦		✦	✦	✦			✦		Exercise course, nature center.

NEW JERSEY

Burlington County

County parks: (609) 267-3300

Facility	Playground	Pool	Lake/Pond	Fishing	Boat Rental	Bike Paths	Bridle Paths	Snack Bar	Grills	Camping	Ice Skating	Sledding	Other
Bass River State Forest Box 118 New Gretna, NJ 08224 (609) 296-1114 18,284 acres	✓	✓	✓	✓		✓	✓	✓	✓	✓	✓	✓	Nature programs, Pine Barrens.
Lebanon State Forest P.O. Box 215 New Lisbon, NJ 08064 (609) 726-1190 29,661 acres	✓	✓	✓						✓	✓	✓	✓	Pine Barrens.
Penn State Forest Box 118 New Gretna, NJ 08224 (609) 296-1114 3,366 acres			✓			✓							Pine Barrens. (summer only)
Smithville Park Jacksonville-Smithville Road Mount Holly, NJ 08060 (609) 265-5068 250 acres			✓										Nature trails. See also Smithville, p. 50.
Wharton State Forest RD 4 Hammonton, NJ 08037 (609) 561-0024 108,773 acres	✓	✓	✓	✓		✓	✓	✓	✓	✓	✓		Pine Barrens, Batsto Village (see p. 45).

NEW JERSEY
Camden County
County parks: (609) 795-PARK

	Playground	Pool	Lake/Pond	Fishing	Boat Rental	Bike Paths	Bridle Paths	Snack Bar	Grills	Camping	Ice Skating	Sledding	Other
Berlin Park Whitehorse Pike Berlin, NJ 08009 (609) 795-PARK 204 acres	✓		✓										Braille trail, tennis.
Camden Park Near Forest Hill School Central Camden, NJ 08101 (609) 795-PARK 22 acres	✓												Tennis.
Cooper River Park North Park Drive Pennsauken, NJ 08110 (609) 795-PARK 410 acres	✓		✓		✓		✓						Golf, track.
Dudley Grange Park Westfield, Federal & 32nd Sts. Camden, NJ 08101 (609) 795-PARK 20 acres	✓				✓								
Haddon Lake Park King's Highway Haddon Heights, NJ 08035 (609) 795-PARK 84 acres	✓				✓								Basketball, tennis.
New Brooklyn Park New Freedom Road Winslow Township, NJ 08081 (609) 795-PARK 561 acres			✓										

NEW JERSEY
Camden County
(continued)

	Playground	Pool	Lake/Pond	Fishing	Boat Rental	Bike Paths	Bridle Paths	Snack Bar	Grills	Camping	Ice Skating	Sledding	Other
Newton Lake Cuthbert Boulevard Haddon Township, NJ 08035 (609) 795-PARK 105 acres	✦		✦		✦								Golf.
Pennypacker Park Park Boulevard Cherry Hill, NJ 08002 609) 795-PARK 92 acres	✦				✦	✦							
Pyne Point Park 7th and Erie Streets Camden, NJ 08101 (609) 795-PARK 15 acres						✦							
Von Neida Park 29th Street Camden, NJ 08101 (609) 795-PARK 12 acres	✦												
Wallworth and Evans Parks King's Hwy. and Cromwell Ave. Cherry Hill, NJ 08002 (609) 795-PARK 72 acres													
Wiggins Parks Mickel Boulevard Camden, NJ 08101 (609) 795-PARK 21 acres				✦									

NEW JERSEY

Cumberland County

County parks: (609) 451-9208

Gloucester County

County parks: (609) 853-5120

	Playground	Pool	Lake/Pond	Fishing	Boat Rental	Bike Paths	Bridle Paths	Snack Bar	Grills	Camping	Ice Skating	Sledding	Other
Cohanzick Zoo Park Mayor Aitken Drive Bridgeton, NJ 08302 (609) 451-9208 1200 acres	✱		✱	✱	✱	✱	✱	✱			✱		See also p. 159.
Bethel Mill Park Delsea Drive & Bethel Mill Rd. Hurffville, NJ 08080 (609) 589-0047 60 acres	✱				✱		✱	✱					Basketball, tennis.
Greenwich Lake Tomlin Station Road Gibbstown, NJ 08027 (609) 853-5120 50 acres	✱		✱	✱				✱					
Red Bank Battlefield Park 100 Hessian Ave. National Park, NJ 08063 (609) 853-5120 40 acres	✱							✱					National historic site.
Scotland Run Park/Wilson Lake Clayton-Williamstown Rd. Clayton, NJ 08312 (609) 881-0845 900 acres				✱				✱					Nature center

NEW JERSEY

Mercer County
County parks: (609) 989-6530

Salem County
County parks: (609) 935-7510 Ext. 222

	Playground	Pool	Lake/Pond	Fishing	Boat Rental	Bike Paths	Bridle Paths	Snack Bar	Grills	Camping	Ice Skating	Sledding	Other
Mercer County Park Mercerville-Edinburg Rd. West Windsor, NJ 08561 (609) 989-6530 — 2500 acres	✹		✹	✹	✹		✹	✹	✹		✹		Handicapped trail, tennis, 100-acre athletic complex, 300-acre lake.
John A. Roebling Park Schiller Avenue Trenton, NJ 08601 (609) 989-6530 — 257 acres			✹										
Rosedale Park Federal City Road Trenton, NJ 08601 (609) 989-6530 — 472 acres	✹		✹					✹					
Fort Mont State Park Fort Mont Road Salem, NJ 08079 (609) 935-3218 — 104 acres	✹	✹	✹										
Parvin State Park RD 1, Box 374 Elmer, NJ 08318 (609) 692-7039 — 1,125 acres	✹	✹	✹	✹			✹	✹	✹	✹	✹	✹	

PENNSYLVANIA

Berks County
County parks: (215) 372-8939

Park	Playground	Pool	Lake/Pond	Fishing	Boat Rental	Bike Paths	Bridle Paths	Snack Bar	Grills	Camping	Ice Skating	Sledding	Other
Kaercher Creek Park Old US Route 22 Hamburg, PA 19526 185 acres (215) 372-8939	✓		✓						✓	✓			
Tulpehocken Creek Valley Park Box 272, RD 5 Sinking Springs, PA 19608 300 acres (215) 372-8939	✓		✓	✓	✓		✓	✓	✓		✓		Tennis, cross-country skiing, exercise course.

Bucks County
County parks: (215) 757-0571

Park	Playground	Pool	Lake/Pond	Fishing	Boat Rental	Bike Paths	Bridle Paths	Snack Bar	Grills	Camping	Ice Skating	Sledding	Other
Black Ditch Park Millcreek and Bloomsdale Roads Levittown, PA 19058 80 acres (215) 757-0571	✓												
Churchville Park Churchville Lane Churchville, PA 18966 172 acres (215) 757-0571						✓		✓			✓		Nature center (*see also* p. 98).
Core Creek Park Tollgate Road Langhorne, PA 19047 1,185 acres (215) 757-0571	✓		✓	✓	✓	✓	✓	✓	✓	✓	✓	✓	Tennis.

PENNSYLVANIA
Bucks County
(continued)

	Playground	Pool	Lake/Pond	Fishing	Boat Rental	Bike Paths	Bridle Paths	Snack Bar	Grills	Camping	Ice Skating	Sledding	Other
Frosty Hollow Park Newportville Road Levittown, PA 19058 (215) 757-0571 95 acres	✓							✓			✓		Tennis.
Lake Towhee Old Bethlehem Road Applebachsville, PA 18951 (215) 757-0571 501 acres	✓		✓			✓		✓	✓	✓	✓	✓	
Neshaminy State Park 263 Dunk's Ferry Road Bensalem, PA 19020 (215) 639-4538 330 acres	✓		✓				✓	✓					
Nockamixon State Park RD3, Box 125A Quakertown, PA 18951 (215) 538-2151 5,253 acres	✓		✓	✓	✓	✓	✓	✓		✓	✓	✓	
Oxford Valley Park Hood Blvd. & Oxford Valley Road Fairless Hills, PA 19030 (215) 757-0571 225 acres	✓		✓					✓		✓	✓	✓	Golf
Peace Valley Park 230 Creek Road Doylestown, PA 18901 (215) 757-0571 1,500 acres	✓		✓	✓	✓	✓	✓	✓		✓	✓	✓	Nature area.

PENNSYLVANIA

Bucks County

(continued)

	Playground	Pool	Lake/Pond	Fishing	Boat Rental	Bike Paths	Bridle Paths	Snack Bar	Grills	Camping	Ice Skating	Sledding	other
Playwicki Park Maple Ave. (Rte. 213) Langhorne, PA 19047 (215) 757-0571 33 acres	✷		✷					✷			✷		
Queen Anne Park New Falls Road Levittown, PA 19058 (215) 757-0571 169 acres	✷										✷		
Ralph Stover State Park Box 209-L, RR 1 Pipersville, PA 18947 (215) 297-5090 45 acres			✷										
Ringing Rocks Bridgeton Road Upper Black Eddy, PA 18972 (215) 757-0571 65 acres													Geological formation.
Roosevelt State Park Box 615-A, RR1 Upper Black Eddy, PA 18972 (215) 982-5560 727 acres			✷	✷ ✷	✷ ✷			✷					
Silver Lake Park Route 13 and Bath Road Bristol, PA 19007 (215) 757-0571 291 acres	✷		✷					✷		✷ ✷	✷ ✷		Nature area (see also p. 105).

PENNSYLVANIA

Bucks County
(continued)

Park	Other	Sledding	Ice Skating	Camping	Grills	Snack Bar	Bridle Paths	Bike Paths	Boat Rental	Fishing	Lake/Pond	Pool	Playground
Stover Myers Mill Dark Hollow Road Point Pleasant, PA 18950 (215) 757-0571 — 21 acres	Grist mill.		✓										✓
Tinicum Park River Road Upper Black Eddy, PA 18972 (215) 757-0571 — 126 acres			✓	✓	✓	✓					✓		✓
Tohickon Valley Cafferty Road Point Pleasant, PA 18950 (215) 757-0571 — 536 acres	Geological Formation.		✓	✓	✓	✓					✓		✓
Tyler State Park Rte. 413 Bypass and Swamp Road Newtown, PA 18940 (215) 968-2021 — 1711 acres			✓	✓		✓	✓		✓		✓		

Chester County
County parks: (215) 431-6415

Park	Other	Sledding	Ice Skating	Camping	Grills	Snack Bar	Bridle Paths	Bike Paths	Boat Rental	Fishing	Lake/Pond	Pool	Playground
French Creek State Park RD 1, Box 448 Elverson, PA 19520 (215) 582-1514 — 7,800 acres			✓	✓	✓	✓	✓			✓	✓		✓

PENNSYLVANIA

Chester County
(continued)

Park	Playground	Pool	Lake/Pond	Fishing	Boat Rental	Bike Paths	Bridle Paths	Snack Bar	Grills	Camping	Ice Skating	Sledding	Other
Hibernia Park RD 6 Coatesville, PA 19320 (215) 384-0290 700 acres	✓		✓			✓		✓	✓	✓			Hibernia Mansion, cross-country skiing.
Marsh Creek State Park RD 2, Park Road Downingtown, PA 19335 (215) 458-8515 1,705 acres	✓	✓	✓	✓		✓	✓	✓	✓	✓	✓		
Nottingham Park 150 Park Road Nottingham, PA 19362 (215) 932-9195 550 acres	✓				✓	✓	✓	✓	✓				Cross-country skiing.
Valley Forge Nat'l Historic Park Routes 23 and 363 Valley Forge, PA 19481 (215) 783-7700 3,000 acres			✓		✓	✓	✓	✓			✓		See also p. 40.
Warwick Park RD 4 Pottstown, PA 19464 (215) 469-9461 700 acres	✓					✓		✓	✓				Cross-country skiing.

PENNSYLVANIA
Delaware County

County parks: (215) 565-4564

	Playground	Pool	Lake/Pond	Fishing	Bike Paths	Bridle Paths	Snack Bar	Grills	Camping	Ice Skating	Sledding	Other
Clayton Park Granite Mine Road Boothwyn, PA 19061 (215) 565-4564 145 acres	✦											Golf.
Ridley Creek State Park Sycamore Mills Rd. Media, PA 19063 (215) 566-4800 2,606 acres	✦		✦		✦	✦	✦			✦		See Colonial Pennsylvania Plantation, p. 46.
Rose Tree Park 1671 North Providence Road Media, PA 19063 (215) 565-4564 72 acres												Many special events (see Calendar of Events, p. 197).
Smedley Park Baltimore Pike Media, PA 19063 (215) 565-4564 78 acres												
Upland Park 6th Street Upland, PA 19015 (215) 565-4564 61 acres												

PENNSYLVANIA

Lancaster County

County parks: (717) 299-8218

	Playground	Pool	Lake/Pond	Fishing	Boat Rental	Bike Paths	Bridle Paths	Snack Bar	Grills	Camping	Ice Skating	Sledding	Other
D.F. Buchmiller Park Routes 222 and 272 Lancaster, PA 17604 (717) 299-8218 62 acres	✓		✓	✓				✓					Tennis.
Central Park Lancaster, PA 17604 (717) 299-8218 560 acres	✓	✓	✓	✓	✓	✓	✓	✓	✓	✓	✓		Garden of Five Senses, tennis, paved trails.
Chickies Rock Park Columbia, PA 17512 (717) 299-8218 117 acres			✓	✓									
Conewago Trail Park Route 230 Elizabethtown, PA 17022 (717) 299-8218 5½ miles					✓	✓							Hiking trail.

Montgomery County

County parks: (215) 278-3555

	Playground	Pool	Lake/Pond	Fishing	Boat Rental	Bike Paths	Bridle Paths	Snack Bar	Grills	Camping	Ice Skating	Sledding	Other
Evansburg State Park P.O. Box 258 Collegeville, PA 19428 (215) 489-3729 3,349 acres				✓	✓	✓							

PENNSYLVANIA

Montgomery County
(continued)

Park	Playground	Pool	Lake/Pond	Fishing	Boat Rental	Bike Paths	Bridle Paths	Snack Bar	Grills	Camping	Ice Skating	Sledding	Other
Fort Washington State Park 500 Bethlehem Pike Fort Washington, PA 19034 (215) 646-2942 493 acres	✓		✓				✓				✓		
Green Lane Reservoir Park Hill Road Green Lane, PA 18054 (215) 234-4863 2,300 acres			✓	✓		✓		✓			✓		805-acre reservoir.
Lorimer Park 183 Moredon Road Huntingdon Valley, PA 19006 (215) 947-3477 225 acres			✓			✓		✓		✓	✓		
Lower Perkiomen Valley Park Mill Road Oaks, PA 19456 (215) 666-5371 107 acres			✓					✓		✓	✓		Basketball court.
Upper Perkiomen Valley Park Green Lane, PA 18054 (215) 234-4528 530 acres			✓			✓	✓	✓	✓	✓	✓		2 lakes, tennis, showers.
Upper Schuylkill Valley Park 1600 Blackrock Rd. Royersford, PA 19468 (215) 948-5170 91 acres		✓	✓					✓			✓		See also p. 88.

PENNSYLVANIA
Philadelphia County
Fairmount Park System
(215) 686-0001

	Playground	Pool	Lake/Pond	Fishing	Boat Rental	Bike Paths	Bridle Paths	Snack Bar	Grills	Camping	Ice Skating	Sledding	Other
Cobbs Creek Park West Philadelphia — 400 acres	X					X					X	X	Tennis, golf, miniature golf, ice-skating.
Fairmount Park Center City to West Philadelphia — 4,000 acres	X			X	X	X	X					X	Archery, biking, bowling, ice skating, tennis. (See also pg. 21).
Franklin D. Roosevelt Park South Philadelphia — 600 acres	X						X			X			Golf, tennis.
Hunting Park Northeast Philadelphia — 200 acres	X						X						
Pennypack Park Northeast Philadelphia — 1,000 acres	X		X		X	X		X	X			X	Equestrian center, nature center.
Wissahickon Park Northwest Philadelphia — 1,600 acres	X		X			X	X	X	X		X	X	Golf, Andorra Natural Area (see p. 22), Valley Green Inn.

RIDES AND TOURS

Note: These lists are for your convenience. We claim no responsibility, nor do we endorse any company.

Hot Air Ballooning

Brandywine Balloon Adventures
  Box 887, Valley Forge, PA 19481   (215) 933-6952

Bucks County Balloon Adventures
  P.O. Box 51, Quakertown, PA 18951   (215) 538-2209

Great Adventure Balloon Club
  Box 1172, Lancaster, PA 17603   (717) 397-3623

Magical Mystery Flights Inc.
  30 Kern Street, Collingdale, PA 19023   (215) 237-9873

Boat Rides

Coryell's Ferry Boat
  22 South Main Street, New Hope, PA 18938   (215) 862-2050

Liberty Belle Charters, Inc.
  Pier 1 North, Delaware River at Race Street
  Philadelphia, PA 19106   (215) 238-0887

MV Lady Christina Harbor Cruises
  100 South King Street
  Wilmington, DE 19801   (302) 658-4522

New Hope Mule Barge
  P.O. Box 164 (Route 232)
  New Hope, PA 18938   (215) 862-2842

R & S Harbor Tours, Inc.
  Penn's Landing Marina, Delaware River at Lombard Street
  Philadelphia, PA 19106   (215) 928-0972

Spirit of Philadelphia
  Penn's Landing, Delaware River at Spruce Street
  Philadelphia, PA 19106 (215) 923-4962, or 923-4993

The state flower of Delaware
is the peach blossom.

Bus Tours

These tours run approximately 1-2 hours. For information about longer tours, call (215) 636-1666. *See also* Trolley Tours.

ABC Bus and Walking Tour
 2929 Galena Road, Philadelphia, PA 19152   (215) 677-2495

American Heritage Landmark Tours
 139 Grubb Road, Malvern, PA 19355 (215) 647-4030

Amish Country Tours/Dutchland Tours
 Box N, Bird-in-Hand, PA 17505   (717) 392-8622

At Your Service Tours
 Box 390, Devon, PA 19333   (215) 296-2828

Centipede Tours
 1315 Walnut Street
 Philadelphia, PA 19107   (215) 735-3123

Foundation for Architecture
 1 Penn Street at Suburban Station, Suite 1665
 Philadelphia 19103   (215) 569-3187

Philadelphia Tours
 719 Dickinson St., Philadelphia 19147   (215) 271-2999

Tracey Tours/Carol Lines
 4425 Rising Sun Ave., Philadelphia 19140   (215) 457-8660

Horse-Drawn Carriage Tours

Youngsters enjoy the horse as much as the history spiel. With young ones, request a shorter tour—it costs less.

Bucks County:
 (pick up near cannon in center of town)
 Bucks County Carriages, New Hope, PA (215) 862-3582

Lancaster County:
 Abe's Buggy Rides, Bird-in-Hand, PA   (no telephone)
 Ed's Buggy Rides, Strasburg, PA   (717) 687-0360
 Forest Ridge Stables, Paradise, PA   (717) 442-4259

Philadelphia:
 (pick up across street from Independence Hall)
 Ben Franklin Carriages   (215) 634-0545
 Philadelphia Carriage Company   (215) 922-6840
 '76 Carriage Company   (215) 923-8516

Plane and Helicopter Rides

Advance reservations required.

Aero Aviation
North Philadelphia Airport
Ashton and Grant Roads
Philadelphia, PA 19114   (215) 338-3649

Fleet Helicopters
Delaware Avenue and Poplar Street
Philadelphia, PA 19106   (215) 282-4100

Golden Wings
Burlington County Airport
Mount Laurel-Eayerstown Road
Lumberton, NJ 08048   (609) 354-8424

Lincoln Flying Service
North Philadelphia Airport
Ashton and Grant Roads, Philadelphia, PA 19114
(215) 969-1011

Northeast Aviation
North Philadelphia Airport
Ashton and Grant Roads, Philadelphia, PA 19114
(215) 677-5592

Smoketown Airport Aerial Tours
Mabel Avenue, Route 340, Smoketown, PA 17576
(717) 394-6476

Sterling Helicopter
Penn's Landing
Delaware Avenue and Catherine Street
Philadelphia 19147   (215) 271-2510

Turner Airport Aerial Tours
1435 Horsham Road, Ambler, PA 19002
(215) 646-2255

Scenic Train Rides

These are special rides behind steam engines, but even a local train ride is an adventure for a very young child.

Ashland Coal Mine
 See page 183.

Blue Mountain and Reading Railroad
 Box 425, Hamburg, PA 19526
 (215) 921-1442

Hawk Mountain Line
 W.K.& S. Railroad, Box 24, Kempton, PA 19529
 (215) 756-6469

New Hope Steam Railway
 Box 612, Huntingdon Valley, PA 19006
 (215) 862-2707, or 379-2169

Strasburg Railroad
 P.O. Box 96, Route 741, Strasburg, PA 17579
 (717) 687-7522

Wilmington and Western Railroad
 Greenbank Station, Routes 2 and 41, Wilmington, DE 19801
 (302) 998-1930

Trolley Tours

Most of the following tours are part of the Fairmount Park system and run at different times of the year. Call Trolley Information at (215) 879-4044 for schedule. Of those listed below, the Fairmount Park Trolley Tour, (215) 636-1666, is the one we recommend for children of all ages, with unlimited off and on privileges for the curious or the restless.

Art Museum Shuttle, (215) 879-4044
Christmas Tour, (215) 879-4044
Fairmount Park Trolley Tour (215) 636-1666
Germantown Express, (215) 879-4044
Schuylkill Discovery, (215) 879-4044
Town and Country Tours, (215) 879-4044
Penn's Landing Trolley, (215) 627-0807
Hawk Mountain Line (*see* Scenic Train Rides above)

Walking Tours

Not all walking tours are included because the longer ones last too long for most children.

Audio Walk and Tour of Philadelphia
c/o Norman Rockwell Museum
6th and Sansom Streets, Philadelphia 19106
(215) 925-1234

Black History Strolls
339 South 2nd Street, Philadelphia, PA 19106
(215) 923-4136

Centipede Inc.
1315 Walnut Street, Philadelphia, PA 19107
(215) 735-3123

Foundation for Architecture Tours
1 Penn Center at Suburban Station
Philadelphia, PA 19103
(215) 569-3187

Ghost Tours
New Hope, PA 18938
(215) 357-4558

Historic Bridgeton Walking Tour
Routes 49 and 77, Bridgeton, NJ 08302
(609) 451-4802, or 455-3230 ext. 262

Museum Without Walls
Walking tour of public art around the Art Museum.
For information, call (215) 787-5449.

Whenever Tours

Go at your leisure in your own car. Call for maps.

Bucks County Covered Bridges
Bucks County Tourist Commission
152 Swamp Road, Doylestown, PA 18901
(215) 345-4552

Burlington County Historical Loop Tours
Burlington County Cultural and Heritage Commission
49 Rancocas Road, Mount Holly, NJ 08060
(609) 265-5068

The New Jersey Pine Barrens covers
1.1 million acres, extends through
four counties, and encompasses
one-third of the State.

ACTIVE SPORTS

Note: These lists are for your convenience only. We claim no responsibility, nor do we endorse any company.

YMCAs and related organizations offer many parent-tot classes. Consult your local phone directory.

Only sports where adults can participate with children are listed here. "Drop-off" programs are not included.

In Philadelphia, the city Department of Recreation, (215) 686-0150, 686-0001, or 686-3612, has information about teams, tournaments, outings and special events in the following sports: baseball, basketball, bicycling, boating, checkers and chess, fishing, golf, hiking, ice skating, jogging, roller skating, sledding, soccer, softball, swimming, tennis, track and field, volleyball.

Baseball

Almost every township has organized baseball for all ages and stages of development. For extra practice, visit:

Burholme Golf
(batting cages)
401 W. Cottman Avenue
Philadelphia, PA
(215) 742-2380

Grand Slam USA
800 Primos Avenue
Folcroft, PA 19032
(215) 586-6622

Grand Slam USA
(indoor batting cages)
Lancaster Pike and Route 29
Frazer, PA
(215) 647-6622

US Golf (batting cages)
7900 City Line Avenue
Philadelphia, PA
(215) 879-3536

Biking

American Youth Hostels
35 South 3rd Street
Philadelphia, 19106
(215) 925-6004

Brandywine Bicycle Club
RD 8, Box 376
Coatesville, PA 19320
(215) 486-0344

New Horizon's Bike Adventures
3495 Horizon Drive
Lancaster, PA 17601
(717) 285-7607

Bicycle Coalition
P.O. Box 8194
Philadelphia, PA 19101
(215) BICYCLE

Fairmount Park Bike Rentals
Kelly Dr. at the Art Museum
Philadelphia, PA 19131
(215) 236-4359

Bowling

Consult your local telephone directory.

Canoeing/Tubing

Canoes are available at all sites; rentals are by the ½ day or full day. Inner tubes available where marked *

Brandywine River:
* Northbrook Canoe, West Chester, PA (215) 793-2279

Delaware River:
* Pt. Pleasant Canoe, Pt. Pleasant, PA (215) 297-8823
* Wilderness Canoe Trips, Wilmington, DE (302) 654-2227

Schuylkill River:
Public Canoe House, Philadelphia, PA (215) 225-3560

New Jersey Pine Barrens:
* Bel Haven Lake, Egg Harbor   (609) 965-2031
* Forks Landing Marina, Hammonton   (609) 561-4337
  Mick's Canoe Rental, Chatsworth   (609) 726-1380
  Paradise Lakes Campground, Hammonton   (609) 561-7095
  Pine Barrens Canoe Rental, Chatsworth   (609) 726-1515
  Wading Pines Campgrounds, Chatsworth   (609) 726-1313

Golf

Young children often prefer miniature golf and putting courses. These places offer miniature golf, putting, and driving ranges; check your local phone directory for others.

Burholme Golf
401 W. Cottman Avenue
Philadelphia, PA
(215) 742-2380

US Golf
7900 City Line Avenue
Philadelphia, PA
(215) 879-3536

City of Philadelphia Public Courses:

Byrne Golf Course
9500 Leon Street
Philadelphia, PA 19114
(215) 632-8666

Cobbs Creek Golf Course
72nd & Lansdowne
Philadelphia, PA 19151
(215) 877-8707

Juniata Golf Course
L & Cayuga Streets
Philadelphia PA 19124
(215) 743-4060

Roosevelt Golf Course
20th Street & Pattison Ave.
Philadelphia, PA 19145
(215) 462-8997

Walnut Lane Golf Course
Walnut Ln. & Magdalena St.
Philadelphia, PA 19128
(215) 482-3370

Horseback Riding

Pony rides are available at the Philadelphia Zoo and Quarry Valley Farm.

Ashford Farms, Inc.
  River Road
  Miquon, PA 19452
  (215) 825-9838

Buttonwood Stables
  Hilliards Bridge Road
  Vincentown, NJ 08088
  (609) 859-0101

Chadds Ford Equestrian Ctr.
  166-B Brinton's Bridge Rd.
  Chadds Ford, PA 19317
  (215) 388-1789

Clover Leaf Acres
  Little Gloucester Road
  Blackwood, NJ 08012
  (609) 227-2111

Discover Adventure
  25 Oregon Avenue
  Mount Laurel, NJ 08054
  (609) 235-7195

Forest Ridge Stables
  Paradise, PA 17562
  (717) 442-4259

Gateway Stables
  Merrybell Lane
  Kennett Square, PA 19348
  (215) 444-9928

Great Valley Stables
  Great Valley Farm, RD 1
  Berwyn, PA 19312
  (215) 296-7492

Holly Oak Farm
  Delsea Drive
  Franklinville, NJ 08322
  (609) 694-1722

Lucky C Stables
  Church Road
  Mount Laurel, NJ 08054
  (609) 234-6550

Rolling Acres Riding School
  207 Atsion Road
  Indian Mills, NJ 08088
  (609) 268-0414

The Other Place
  Tuckerton Road
  Indian Mills, NJ 08088
  (609) 268-0038

Thorncroft Equestrian Center
  Line and Boot Roads
  Malvern, PA 19355
  (215) 644-1963

  (Excellent programs for
  handicapped riders)

Ice Skating

These rinks are open to the public. Call for hours:

Cobbs Creek Rink
63rd and Walnut Street
Philadelphia 19039
(215) 748-3480

Coliseum
333 Preston Avenue
Voorhees, NJ 08043
(609) 429-3511

Evesham Skating Center Inc.
Evesboro-Medford Road
Marlton, NJ 08053
(609) 983-3500

Rizzo Rink
Front and Washington
Philadelphia, PA 19047
(215) 686-2925

Scanlan Recreation Center
J and Cayuga Streets
Philadelphia, PA 19034
(215) 739-5515

Simon's
Walnut Lane and Woolfton
Philadelphia, PA 19138
(215) 924-8297

Skating Club of Wilmington
Carruthers Lane
Wilmington, DE 19803
(302) 656-5005

Skatium
Darby and Manoa Roads
Havertown, PA 19083
(215) 853-2225

Wissahickon Ice Skating Club
Willow Grove and Cherokee, Philadelphia 19118
(215) 247-1907

League Sports

Little League Baseball, Softball, Football, Soccer and other sports flourish throughout the area. Contact your township Recreation Director or Civic Association for information.

Roller Skating

CN Skate Palace Ltd.
247 Concord Road
Easton, PA 19014
(215) 494-4442

Cherry Hill Skating Center
Old Cuthbert and Deer Rds.
Cherry Hill, NJ 08034
(609) 795-1919

Cornwell's Roller Skating
2350 Bristol Pike
Cornwell Heights, PA 19020
(215) 638-7766

Deptford Skating Center
Cedar and Deptford Avenue
Deptford, NJ 08096
(609) 845-7353

Elmwood Roller Skating Rink
2406 South 71st Street
Philadelphia 19142
(215) 492-8543

Young's Regency Skating Ctr.
650 Skippack Pike (Rte. 73)
Blue Bell, PA 19422
(215) 643-7888

Skiing: Downhill

Big Boulder
Lake Harmony, PA 18624
(717) 722-0101

Chadds Peak
Chadds Ford, PA 19317
(215) 388-2381

Doe Mountain
Macungie, PA 18062
(215) 682-7109

Elk Mountain
Union Dale, PA 18470
(717) 679-2611

Jack Frost
White Haven, PA 18661
(215) 443-8425

Little Gap
Palmerton, PA 18071
(215) 826-7700

Montage
Taylor, PA 18518
(717) 969-7669

Roundtop
Lewisburg, PA 17837
(717) 432-9631

Shawnee
Shawnee-on-Delaware 18356
(717) 421-7231

Split Rock
Lake Harmony, PA 18624
(717) 722-9111

Spring Mountain
Schwenksville, PA 19473
(215) 287-7900

Camelback Mountain
Tannersville, PA 18372
(717) 629-1661

Skiing: Cross Country

See also page 137 for trails in county and state parks.

Camp Speers
Dingman's Ferry, PA 18328
(717) 828-2329

Hanley's Happy Hill
Eagles Mere, PA 17731
(717) 525-3461

Jack Frost Mountain
White Haven, PA 18661
(717) 443-8425

Ridley Creek State Park
Media, PA 19063
(215) 566-4800

Swimming

For the nearest pools, contact your neighborhood YMCA or
your township Recreation Department.

Tennis

Many neighborhood parks have public courts. Call your township Recreation Department for information.

Arthur Ashe Youth Tennis Center (indoor tennis, Oct.-April)
4015 Main Street, Philadelphia, PA 19127
(215) 487-9555

SPECTATOR SPORTS

Professional and Division I College teams are listed for 28 sports. The number in parenthesis after each college stadium name indicates seating capacity. Until hero-worship and team loyalties become a factor, consider taking a young child to a college game where the crowds aren't overwhelming and the child can sit close to the action. Pro Information is listed with each sport.

For college sports information and game schedules, call:
Drexel University, Philadelphia, PA (215) 895-2550
Lafayette College, Easton, PA (215) 250-5470
La Salle University, Philadelphia, PA (215) 951-1516
Lehigh University, Bethlehem, PA (215) 758-3174
Philadelphia College of Textiles
   and Science, Philadelphia, PA (215) 951-2852
St. Joseph's University, Philadelphia, PA (215) 879-7450
Temple University, Philadelphia, PA (215) 787-7445
University of Delaware, Newark, DE (302) 451-2186
University of Pennsylvania, Philadelphia, PA (215) 898-6128
Villanova University, Villanova, PA (215) 645-4120

Baseball

Pro:
Philadelphia Phillies: (April-October)
   Veteran's Stadium (64,000)
   Broad and Pattison Streets, Philadelphia, PA 19145
   (215) 463-1000

Every Sunday home game is a Give Away Day with caps and other freebies that kids love.

College: (spring)
MEN: Drexel, Lafayette, La Salle, Lehigh, St. Joseph's, Temple, University of Delaware, University of Pennsylvania, Villanova.
WOMEN: *See* Softball.

Basketball

Pro: (November-April)
Philadelphia '76ers
  Spectrum (18,000)
  Broad and Pattison Streets
  Philadelphia, PA 19145
  (215) 339-7676
  Call for special give-away days.

The Harlem Globetrotters come for one weekend in February or March. Call Spectrum, (215) 339-7676, for schedule.

College: (winter)
MEN: Drexel, Physical Education Center (2,500)
Lafayette, Kirby Fieldhouse (3,500)
La Salle, the Palestra (8,700)
Lehigh, Stabler Center (5,800)
Rollin' Owls Wheelchair Team, Temple (215) 787-6976
St. Joseph's, Alumni Fieldhouse (3,100)
Temple, McGonigle Hall (4,500)
University of Delaware, Delaware Fieldhouse (2,300)
University of Pennsylvania, the Palestra (8,700)
Villanova, DuPont Pavilion (6,500)
WOMEN: La Salle, Hayman Hall (1,000)

Boxing

Pro: For information, call the Spectrum (215) 389-5000.

College: No Division I teams.

Crew

Club: (May through early fall)
Schuylkill Navy: ten private clubs which often practice *early* mornings and weekends. For information call Fairmount Park, (215) 686-0001. Regattas May-July.

College: (March to early May)
MEN and WOMEN: Drexel, La Salle, Temple, University of Pennsylvania. All crews row on the Schuylkill River starting at Boathouse Row.

Cricket

Club: (spring)
Prior Cricket Club (215) 878-2552
Haverford College (215) 896-1000

Cross-Country

College:
See Track and Field, page 157.

Fencing

College: (winter)
MEN: University of Pennsylvania.
WOMEN: Temple, University of Pennsylvania.

Field Hockey

College: (fall)
WOMEN: Drexel, Lafayette, La Salle, Lehigh, St. Joseph's,
Temple, University of Delaware, University of Pennsylvania,
Villanova.

Football

Pro: (August-December)
Philadelphia Eagles
    Veterans Stadium (65,000)
    Broad and Pattison
    Philadelphia, PA 19145
    (215) 463-5500

College: (fall, men only)
Army-Navy Game, JFK Stadium (102,000). For information,
    call West Point, NY (914) 446-4996.
Lafayette, Fisher Field (13,500)
Lehigh, Murray H. Goodman Stadium (14,000)
Temple, Veterans Stadium (66,600)
University of Delaware, Delaware Stadium (22,000)
University of Pennsylvania, Franklin Field (60,000)
Villanova, Villanova Stadium (13,400)

Golf

College: (spring)
MEN: Drexel, Lafayette, La Salle, Lehigh, St. Joseph's, Temple,
University of Delaware, Villanova.
WOMEN: Lehigh.
Call for location of golf courses.

Gymnastics

College: (winter)
MEN: Temple
WOMEN: Temple, University of Pennsylvania

Horse Shows

(spring through fall)
See local media or Calendar of Events.

Ice Hockey

Pro: (September-April)
Philadelphia Flyers
   Spectrum (17,400)
   Broad and Pattison Streets
   Philadelphia, PA 19145
   (215) 465-4500

   Call for special Give-Away Days.

College: (winter)
MEN: Villanova.

Ice Skating

Check local media or Calendar of Events for ice shows.

Lacrosse

Pro: (December-February)
Wings
   Spectrum   (17,4000)
   Broad and Pattison Streets
   Philadelphia, PA 19145
   (215) 336-3600

College: (spring)
MEN: Drexel, Lafayette, Lehigh, University of Delaware, University of Pennsylvania, Villanova.
WOMEN: Drexel, Lafayette, Lehigh, Temple, University of Delaware, University of Pennsylvania, Villanova.

Riflery

College: Winter
MEN and WOMEN: Lehigh.

Rodeo

Pro: (Memorial Day-Labor Day, Saturday 7:30 PM)
Cowtown Rodeo
   Woodstown, NJ
   (609) 769-3200, or 769-3207

Rowing

See Crew

Rugby

Club: (spring)
Black Thorn Rugby Club, (215) 441-8424.
Brandywine Rugby Club, (215) 696-0722.
Doylestown Rugby Club, (215) 348-2185.
Philadelphia Whitemarsh, (215) 489-6790.
Second City Troop, (215)-431-3998.
South Jersey Rugby Club, (609)-795-4406.

Soccer

College: (fall)
MEN: Drexel, Lafayette, La Salle, Lehigh, Philadelphia College
of Textiles and Science, St. Joseph's, Temple, University of
Delaware, University of Pennsylvania, Villanova.
WOMEN: La Salle, Villanova.

Softball

College: (spring)
WOMEN: Drexel, Lafayette, La Salle, Lehigh, St. Joseph's,
Temple, University of Delaware, University of Pennsylvania,
Villanova.

Squash

College: (winter)
MEN and WOMEN: University of Pennsylvania.

Swimming

College: (winter)
MEN and WOMEN: Drexel, Lafayette, La Salle, Lehigh,
University of Delaware, University of Pennsylvania.

Tennis

Pro: Check local media or Calendar of Events for tournaments.

College:
MEN: Drexel (spring), Lafayette (fall and spring), La Salle (spring), Lehigh (fall and spring), St. Joseph's (fall), Temple (fall and spring), University of Delaware (spring), University of Pennsylvania (fall and spring), Villanova (fall and spring).
WOMEN: Drexel (spring), Lafayette (fall and spring), La Salle, (fall), Lehigh (fall and spring), St. Joseph's (spring), Temple (fall and spring), University of Delaware (fall), University of Pennsylvania (fall and spring), Villanova (fall).

Track and Field

College: (fall, winter, spring; indoor and outdoor)
MEN and WOMEN: Drexel, Lafayette, La Salle, Lehigh, St. Joseph's, Temple, University of Delaware, University of Pennsylvania, Villanova.

Don't miss the Penn Relays in April.

Volleyball

College: (fall)
WOMEN only: Drexel, Lafayette, La Salle, Lehigh, Temple, University of Delaware, University of Pennsylvania.

Water Polo

College: (winter)
MEN: Villanova.

Wrestling

Pro:
Call the Spectrum, (215) 389-5000, for information

College: (winter)
MEN: Drexel, La Salle, Lehigh, University of Delaware, University of Pennsylvania, Villanova.

Unique Areas

A few areas deserve to have their own section because they have so much to offer all in one place.

Bridgeton, New Jersey, is the state's largest historic district with 2200 registered National Historic Sites!

Germantown is a section of Philadelphia known for its historic buildings, as the site of an important Revolutionary War battle, and as the location of stations on the Underground Railroad that brought slaves to freedom in the North.

Hershey, Pennsylvania, is a fine example of how a single, caring company can help develop different resources within a town.

Lancaster, Pennsylvania, is famous for the kind hospitality offered by members of its Amish, Mennonite and Hutterite communities. Magnificent countryside provides a scenic background for the farms open to the public and the numerous railroad and farm vehicle museums that children love.

BRIDGETON, NEW JERSEY

Driving: From Philadelphia, take Ben Franklin or Walt Whitman Bridge to I-676 south. Follow I-676 to Rte. 130 south to Rte. 45 south to Rte. 77 south. Continue along Rte. 77 south into the town of Bridgeton. Go left on West Commerce Street, then left onto Aitken Drive. Individual directions for highlights follow.

Tours/Programs: The Bridgeton-Cumberland Tourist Association (Routes 49 and 77) offers bus and trolley tours and cassette tapes for walking tours of historic Bridgeton. (609) 451-4802.

Bridgeton highlights with special appeal for children:

Cohanzick Zoo

Bridgeton, NJ 08302
(609) 455-3230 (City Hall), ext. 242

Hours: Dawn to dusk.

Cost: Free.

Description: Small zoo in the City of Bridgeton Park features birds and small primates. Local animals include fox, raccoon and skunk. Large mammals range from black bear and mountain lion to zebra.

Time Needed: 30 minutes.

Eating: OK in Park, not in Zoo.

Driving: When you enter Bridgeton on Rte. 77 south, turn right at the light onto Washington Street. At dead end go right, enter Park and watch for signs.

Codes: 🦽 🚐 🪶

New Jersey's nickname
is the Garden State.

Hall of Fame Sports Museum

Babe Ruth Drive and Burt Street
Bridgeton, NJ 08302
(609) 451-7300

Hours: Monday-Friday 10 AM-12 Noon and 1-3 PM. Closed weekends and holidays.

Cost: Free.

Description: Extensive collection of local and national sports memorabilia. Trophy Room has famous cups and awards from baseball, boxing, football and the Olympics. Photos, uniforms, bats and balls from local teams, the Philadelphia Phillies and the Cincinnati Reds.

Time Needed: 30-90 minutes.

Driving: From Bridgeton's Aitken Drive, follow signs for the Recreation Center. Take the first left onto Babe Ruth Drive, Museum is at the next corner, Babe Ruth Drive and Burt Street.

Codes: &. 🏇

Nail House Museum

1 Aitken Drive
Bridgeton, NJ 08302
(609) 455-4100

Hours: April-December, Tuesday-Friday 10:30 AM-3:30 PM, Saturday-Sunday 11 AM-4 PM.

Cost: Free, donations appreciated.

Description: 19th-century men and boys labored here to make iron nails used throughout the United States. Tools of the trade and an old waterpowered nail machine on display. Check the Nail Master's desk and its secret drawer lined with the original newspaper announcing Lincoln's death.

Time Needed: 30 minutes.

Driving: Museum is immediately on your right as you turn onto Aitken Drive from West Commerce Street.

Codes: &. 🏇

Woodruff Indian Museum

Bridgeton Free Public Library
East Commerce Street
Bridgeton, NJ 08302
(609) 451-2620

Hours: Monday-Thursday 9 AM-12 Noon and 2-4 PM, Saturday 10 AM-12 Noon and 2-4 PM. Closed Sunday.

Cost: Free.

Description: More than 2000 artifacts have been donated to the Museum, including arrowheads, pieces of clay pots, beads, smoking pipes and other items used by the Nanicoke Lenni-Lenape Indians native to the area.

Time Needed: 45 minutes.

Driving: Follow Rte. 77 south to Bridgeton, then turn right onto East Commerce Street.

Codes: ♿ 🦖

New Jersey is the most
densely populated state
in the Union.

GERMANTOWN, PHILADELPHIA

Driving: With a street map of Philadelphia in your pocket, take I-76 (Schuylkill Expressway) west to the Lincoln Drive exit. Follow Lincoln Drive till it dead ends at Allen's Lane. Turn right to Germantown Avenue. From here, your street map will be useful.

Awbury Arboretum

Chew Avenue at Washington Lane
Germantown, PA 19144
(215) 849-2855 (City Parks Association)

Hours: Dawn to dusk.

Cost: Free.

Description: 57 acres in Germantown provide ample space to appreciate nature and the legacy of the Cope family. One 250-year-old black oak tree is older than our country. Please note that some of the houses are private residences and not open to the public.

Codes: ♿ 🚐

Cliveden

6401 Germantown Avenue
Philadelphia, PA 19144
(215) 848-1777

Hours: April-December, Tuesday-Saturday 10 AM-4 PM, Sunday 1:30-4:30 PM.

Cost: $3.00 adults, $1.50 children.

Description: Elegant furniture and memorabilia from more than 200 years of Chew family history have been kept in this historic house museum. Young visitors enjoy the family's treasures and trivia along with the scars left on the building from the Battle of Germantown on October 4, 1777.

Tours/Programs: Tours on the hour, good programs for school groups.

Eating: Indoor and outdoor picnic facilities.

Codes: ♿ 🚻 🚐 👶

Concord Schoolhouse

6313 Germantown Avenue
Philadelphia, PA 19144

Description: One room schoolhouse in the corner of Germantown's Upper Burying Ground. Records and trustee meeting minutes have been kept since 1776. Original furniture, lanterns, desks and books reflect the sparse simplicity of this strict schoolroom, where learning was a privilege and unruly students were not allowed to attend. Visits by appointment only; call (215) 438-6328.

Deshler-Morris House

5442 Germantown Avenue
Philadelphia, PA 19144
(215) 596-1748

Hours: April-December, Tuesday-Sunday 1-4 PM.

Cost: $.50.

Description: Known as the "Germantown White House" because George Washington lived here from 1793-1794 to escape the yellow fever plaguing Philadelphia (at that time, Philadelphia was the capital of the country.). The President's bedroom is on the second floor front.

Codes: 🦌 🚐

Ebenezer Maxwell Mansion

200 West Tulpehocken Street
Philadelphia, PA 19144
(215) 438-1861

Hours: April-December, Wednesday-Sunday 1-4 PM.

Cost: $2.00 adults, $1.00 children and senior citizens.

Description: Wonderful Victorian architecture and use of wrought iron. Guided tours tell about the roles of parents, children and servants in the mid-19th century. Children may try out antique toys and household items.

Tours/Programs: Very good programs encourage children to compare family lifestyles as well as neighboring architectural styles. Role-playing opportunities for school groups. Weekly summer programs for children.

Codes: 🦌 🚐

Germantown Historical Society Museum Complex

5214 Germantown Avenue
Philadelphia, PA 19144
(215) 844-0514

Hours: Tuesday and Thursday 10 AM-4 PM, Sunday 1-5 PM.
Closed major holidays.

Cost: $2 adults, $1.50 students, under 6 free.

Description: Museum complex includes:
Baynton House: library, archives on local and regional history.
Clarkson-Watson House: costume museum has everything
    from tiny baby bonnets to fancy ball gowns, from Quaker
    simplicity to high fashion.
Conyngham-Hacker House: orientation center for overview of
    Germantown, decorative arts museum , display of items
    donated by early generations of Germantown families.
Howell House: museum of toys, puzzles, dolls and doll furni-
    ture, quilts and samplers. Watch for Belsnickle, a German
    version of Santa Claus.
Von Trott Museum Annex: 18th-century horse-drawn sleighs,
    tools and implements of rural living.

Tours/Programs: One hour tour (no wandering alone).

Eating: Picnics possible on the lawn.

Codes: 🦌 🚐

Germantown Mennonite Information Center

6117 Germantown Avenue
Philadelphia, PA 19144
(215) 843-0943

Hours: Tuesday-Saturday 10 AM-4 PM. Closed Thanksgiving
weekend, Christmas, New Year's Day.

Cost: Free.

Description: Site of the first Mennonite Church in the colonies. First recorded protest against slavery signed here in
1688. See Johnson House, below.

Codes: 🦌 🚐

Grumblethorpe

5267 Germantown Avenue
Philadelphia, PA 19144
(215) 843-4820

Hours: April-December, Saturday 1-4 PM.

Cost: $2.00 adults, $1.00 children.

Description: Furnished house and garden.

Codes: 🕎 🚐

Johnson House

6306 Germantown Avenue
Philadelphia, PA 19144
(215) 843-0943

Hours: April-December, Saturday 1-4 PM.

Cost: $2.00 adults, $1.00 children.

Description: 18th-century Mennonite house and garden. Germantown was a stop along the Underground Railroad that helped slaves fleeing from bondage. Quaker and Mennonite religious beliefs "knew slavery to be a sin against God" and aided fugitive slaves in their flight to freedom.

Codes: 🕎 🚐

Loudon

4650 Germantown Avenue
Philadelphia, PA 19144
(215) 842-2877

Hours: April-December, Sunday 1-4 PM.

Cost: $2.00 adults, $1.00 children.

Description: Collections of five generations of one family.

Codes: 🕎 🚐

Paley Design Center

Philadelphia College of Textiles and Science
4200 Henry Avenue
Philadelphia, PA 19144
(215) 951-2860

Hours: Tuesday-Saturday 10 AM-4 PM.

Cost: Free.

Description: Ethnic costumes, children's clothes nearly 100 years old, collections of feathers, fabrics, shoes, shells and hundreds of other colorful designs. Most in storage and can be retrieved by appointment for interested students. Exhibit Hall open to the public.

Codes:

Stenton

18th and Windrim Streets
Philadelphia, PA 19144
(215) 329-7312

Hours: February-December, Tuesday-Saturday 1-4 PM.

Cost: $2.00 adults, $1.00 children.

Description: Washington used this building as headquarters, but children are usually more interested in the restored barn, orangery and weaving shed.

Codes:

Upsala

6430 Germantown Avenue
Philadelphia, PA 19144
(215) 842-1798

Hours: April-December, Tuesday and Thursday 1-4 PM.

Cost: $2.00 adults, $1.00 children.

Description: Washington's soldiers placed their cannons on Upsala's lawns to blast the British occupying Cliveden across the street.

Codes:

Woodmere Art Museum

9201 Germantown Avenue
Philadelphia, PA 19118
(215) 247-0476

Hours: Tuesday-Saturday 10 AM-5 PM, Sunday 2-5 PM.
Closed Mondays, holidays, weekends in July and August.

Cost: $2.00 donation requested.

Description: Museum collection blends historical and cultural artifacts. Children's Gallery has work done by children for other children to view. Many art classes for children and adults throughout the year.

Time Needed: ½   hour.

Tours/Programs: Call for children's classes.

Codes: 🛫 🚐 👫

Wyck

6026 Germantown Avenue
Philadelphia, PA 19144
(215) 848-1690

Hours: April-December, Tuesday, Thursday and Saturday 1-4 PM.

Cost: $2.00 adults, $1.00 children.

Description: 1689, oldest family home in Germantown. Special gardens developed and still maintained.

Codes: 🛫 🚐

HERSHEY, PENNSYLVANIA

Hershey, "Chocolate Town, U.S.A."

Information: Hershey's Visitors Center
400 West Hershey Park Drive
Hershey, PA 17033
(717) 534-3005, or (800) 533-3131

Individual costs listed under each attraction. To reach any
exhibit, it's best to follow directions to main parking lot of Visitors Center, then take the appropriate tram to each attraction. Reach Zoo by car; no tram from parking lot.
Accommodations include hotels, motels and campgrounds.

Eating: Best in Park and Chocolate World. Picnic tables scattered throughout, covered tables near parking lot.

Driving: Take PA Turnpike west to Exit 20. Follow Rte. 72
north to Rte. 322 west to Hershey.

Codes: ♿ ✈ 🚗 ⛵

Chocolate World

Hershey, PA 17033
(717) 534-4900

Hours: Monday-Saturday 9 AM-4:45 PM, Sundays 12 Noon-
4:45 PM.

Cost: Free.

Description: Visitors sit in vehicles that wind through a lively exhibit describing the story of chocolate—from beans in
tropical forests to candy bars and cocoa. It's hard to resist the
huge sundaes at the Dessert Cafe!

Hershey Gardens

Hershey, PA 17033
(717) 534-3492

Hours: April-October, daily 9 AM-5 PM; Memorial Day-Labor
Day, daily 9 AM-7 PM.

Cost: $3.00 adults, $1.00 children 4-18, under 4 free.

Description: 23 acres of colorful, fragrant flowers, shrubs
and trees. Massed plantings of 50,000 tulips in April,
14,000 roses in June, and 13,000 annuals all summer are just
three of the impressive displays.

Hershey Museum of American Life

Hershey, PA 17033
(717) 534-3439

Hours: Memorial Day-Labor Day, daily 10 AM-6 PM; Labor Day-Memorial Day, daily 10 AM-5 PM. Closed Thanksgiving, Christmas, New Year's Day.

Cost: $3.00 adults, $1.25 children 4-18, under 4 free.

Description: Founder Milton Hershey's memorabilia and "Adam Danner's World" with mini-exhibits to tell about Pennsylvania German life in the early 1800s. Also, American Indian and Eskimo artifacts, antique fire engines, Conestoga wagons, rifles and tableware. Children's Activity Area has scheduled events with wide appeal.

Hersheypark

Hershey, PA 17033
(717) 534-3900

Hours: Mid-April to September, opens 10:30 AM daily, closing time varies between 6 and 10 PM. Open one weekend in October. Open for Christmas week special.

Cost: $16.75 ages 9 and up, $13.75 children 4-8.

Description: 87 acres and dozens of rides for all ages. Adventuresome big kids go right to Canyon River Rapids or the Comet. Little ones prefer the carousel, the coal cracker or a cool paddleboat ride. Live entertainment under the trees throughout the park.

Zoo America

North American Wildlife Park
Hershey, PA 17033
(717) 534-3860

Hours: Daily, 10 AM-various closing times daily. Closed Thanksgiving, Christmas and New Year's.

Cost: $3.00 adults, $1.75 children 4-18, under 3 free.

Description: Animals and plants from five regions of North America. Alligators, black bears, elk and bison. More than 200 animals in spacious eleven-acre park setting.

LANCASTER, PENNSYLVANIA

Children of the Electronic Eighties find a very different life-style in this gentle rolling farm country: no TV, no video games, often no electricity. One-room schoolhouses still used today, distinct black carriages in place of cars, and respect for each other reflect the Amish, Mennonite and Hutterite beliefs.

Driving: From Philadelphia, go west on Rte. 30; OR: PA Turnpike to Rte. 100 south to Rte. 30 west. The majority of attractions listed are along Rte. 30 *before* the city of Lancaster. *See* Lancaster map, page 231.

Pennsylvania Dutch Visitors Bureau

501 Greenfield Road
Lancaster, PA 17601
(717) 299-8901

Hours: Daily 8 AM-8 PM.

Description: Information on all Lancaster places and events. 36-minute film called *The Lancaster Experience* explains the history and heritage of the area and its people, highlighting events such as barn-raising and the tragedy of a barn fire in this agricultural community.
Movie hours: January-February, by appointment only; March, Saturday-Sunday 10 AM-3 PM on the hour; April-November, daily 9 AM-4 PM on the hour; December, Saturday 10 AM-3 PM on the hour.

Codes: ♿ ✝ 🚐

Amish Farm and House

2395 Lincoln Highway East (Rte. 30)
Lancaster, PA 17602
(717) 394-6185

Hours: November-March, daily 8:30 AM-4 PM; April-May, September-October, daily 8:30 AM-5 PM; June, July, August, daily 8:30-6 PM.

Cost: $3.90 adults, $2.00 children 5-11, under 5 free.

Description: Farm has everything from hatching eggs to tobacco crops. Ride in an old Conestoga wagon, built in the early 1700's. Visit the secondary museum to see collections of local Indian artifacts, children's toys and dolls. Foreign-language tours available.

Eating: Covered picnic area.

Codes: ♿ 🚐

Amish Homestead

2034 Lincoln Highway East
Lancaster, PA 17602
(717) 392-0832

Hours: Daily 9 AM-4 PM.

Cost: $3.75 ages 12 and over, $1.75 children 6-11, under 5 free.

Description: "The only occupied Amish farm open consistently to tourists." Spring and summer best for seeing piglets, lambs, etc. on this large, 71-acre dairy farm.

Codes: 🚐

Amish Village

Route 896, P.O. Box 115
Strasburg, PA 17579
(717) 687-8511

Hours: Spring and fall, daily 9 AM-5 PM; summer, daily 9 AM-6 PM.

Cost: $3.85 ages 13 and over, $4.40 children 6-12.

Description: Guided house tour takes approximately 30-40 minutes, but more time needed to see blacksmith shop, operating smokehouse and water wheel, farm animals and one-room schoolhouse.

Codes: ♿ 🚐

Anderson Bakery

2060 Old Philadelphia Pike (Route 340)
Lancaster, PA 17602
(717) 299-2321

Hours: Monday-Friday 8:30 AM-3 PM.

Cost: Free.

Description: Walk along the glass-enclosed catwalk above a fully automated pretzel factory. Twenty minute self-guided tour shows dough being mixed, pretzels formed, baked and packaged.

Codes: 🐴 🚐

Candy Americana Museum/Wilbur Chocolates

46 North Broad Street
Lititz, PA 17543
(717) 626-1131

Hours: Monday-Saturday 10 AM-5 PM.

Cost: Free.

Description: Exhibit shows how candy was made by hand in the past plus many candy molds in different shapes.

Codes: 🔧

Choo-Choo Barn

Route 741 East, Box 130
Strasburg, PA 17579
(717) 687-7911

Hours: April, November and December, Saturday-Sunday 11 AM-5 PM; May, September and October, daily 10 AM-5 PM; June, July and August, daily 10 AM-6 PM.

Cost: $2.50 adults over 12, $1.00 children 5-12.

Description: Giant layout of O-gauge model trains running through and around villages and mountains. Real waterfalls, a circus, fire engines putting out a house on fire, a total of 125 animated objects. Day and night scenes.

Codes: ♿ 🔧 🚐

Dutch Wonderland

2249 Route 30 East
Lancaster, PA 17602
(717) 291-1888

Hours: Easter Weekend-Memoril Day, Saturday 10 AM-6 PM, Sunday 12 Noon-6 PM; Memorial Day-Labor Day, Saturday 10 AM-7 PM, Sunday 11 AM-7 PM; day after Labor Day-October, Saturday 10 AM-6 PM, Sunday 12 Noon-6 PM.

Cost: $8.05 admission and 5 rides, $11.55 unlimited rides, infants and small toddlers free.

Description: Perfect amusement park for younger children. Boats, cars, trains, double splash roller coaster, high dive demonstration, monorail around the park ($1 extra).

Eating: Concession stands, cafeteria, restaurant.

Codes: ♿ 🚐

Ephrata Cloisters

632 West Main Street
Ephrata, PA 17522
(717) 733-6600

Hours: Monday-Saturday 9 AM-5 PM, Sunday 12 Noon-5 PM.
Closed Mondays December-March, holidays except Memorial
Day, July 4, and Labor Day.

Cost: $3.00 adults, $1.50 children 6-17, under 6 free.

Description: One of America's earliest religious societies
began here in 1732. They built medieval-style buildings and
lived a life of self-denial and discipline. Their important paper
industry (books and broadside printing) has been famous
since 1743 for its beautiful calligraphy and illuminated work.
Examples of their handcrafted furniture, basket making and
unusual music are everywhere. Children are amazed at how
tiny the residents' bedrooms were.

Time Needed: 1½ hours.

Tours/Programs: Must go on 40-minute tour to enter main
building. Vorspiel, a musical drama depicting cloister life and
featuring cloister music, is presented weekend evenings from
July to September.

Eating: Picnics allowed.

Codes: ♿ ✈ 🚍

Philadelphia became the capital of
Pennsylvania in 1790. In 1799 the
state capital was moved to Lancaster
and then to Harrisburg.

Folk Craft Center and Museum

Mount Sidney Road
Witmer, PA 17585
(717) 397-3609

Hours: Monday-Saturday 9 AM-5 PM, Sunday 12 Noon-4 PM.
Closed major holidays.

Cost: Slide Show/Museum: $4.00 adults, $2.00 children 6-14,
under 6 free, $10.00 family.
Slide Show only: $2.00 adults, $1.00 children 6-14, under 6
free, $5.00 family.
Museum only: $3.00 adults, $2.00 children 6-14, under 6 free,
$8.00 family.

Description: Professional slide show spans the different seasons and lifestyles of the Pennsylvania Dutch. Museum gallery
has exhibits on Pennsylvania Dutch folklore, barn-raising,
and "Meet the Mennonites." Great Hall is a replica of a Mennonite house, including walk-in fireplace. In the back, look for
herb garden, woodworker's shed and 1762 Weave Haus with
old beam loom still in use.

Time Needed: 1 hour.

Tours/Programs: 15-minute slide presentation, "The Land
We Love."

Codes: 🐴

Gast Classic Motorcars Exhibit

Route 896, RD 2, Box 1G
Strasburg, PA 17519
(717) 687-9500

Hours: May-October, daily 9 AM-9 PM; November-April,
Sunday-Thursday 9 AM-5 PM, Friday and Saturday
9 AM-9 PM.

Cost: $4.00 ages over 13, $2.00 children 6-12, under 6 free.

Description: Life-sized scrapbook of the automobile. Bright
modern museum has antiques, classics, sports, and celebrity
cars including the DeLorean.

Time Needed: 1-2 hours.

Codes: ♿ 🐴

Hans Herr House

Hans Herr Drive
Lancaster, PA 17602
(717) 464-4438

Hours: April-December, Monday-Saturday 9 AM-4 PM.

Cost: $2.50 adults, $1.00 children 7-12, under 7 free.

Description: Oldest house in Lancaster County (1719); oldest Mennonite Church in North America. Step into the fireplace and look up the chimney; see where the children slept in the attic. Outside look for a full range of farming implements, blacksmith shop, bake oven, smokehouse and apple orchards.

Eating: Picnic tables.

Codes: 👌 ✝ 🚐

Kitchen Kettle Village

Route 340
Intercourse, PA 17534
(717) 768-8261

Hours: All year 'round, Monday-Saturday 9 AM-5 PM. Closed major holidays.

Description: Twenty shops offer local crafts and homebaked treats. Jellies and relishes, baked goods, crafts, candy all made right there.

Lancaster Newspaper Newseum

South Queen Street
Lancaster, PA 17601
(717) 291-8600 (Lancaster Newspapers, Inc.)

Glass-enclosed exhibit on street showing old printing presses with captions explaining use of machines.

Mennonite Heritage Center

24 Main Street
Souderton, PA 18964-1713
(215) 723-1700

Hours: Wednesday-Saturday 10 AM-4 PM, Sunday 2-4 PM.

Cost: Free, donations accepted.

Description: Three centuries of Anabaptist-Mennonite heritage. Strong emphasis on family. Special programs for school groups.

Codes: ✝ 🚐

Mill Bridge Village and Campground

Box 86, Ronks Road
Strasburg, PA 17579
(717) 687-8181

Hours: April 1-end of October, daily 9:30 AM-5:30 PM;
November-December 14, Saturday and Sunday for "Christmas
in the Mill." Winter, closed. Mid-March, campground (only)
opens.

Cost: $5.90 adults, $3.50 children 6-12, under 6 free.

Description: Free Amish buggy rides with paid admission.
Visit the 1738 Mill, still operating, with an exhibit upstairs. In
the Village, watch broom makers at work, visit shops and
craftspeople. Campground welcomes all campers—tents to
RVs, and has old-fashioned playground for children.

Codes: ♿ 🚐

National Wax Museum

Route 30
Lancaster, PA 17602
(717) 393-3679

Hours: Daily 9 AM-9 PM.

Cost: $3.65 adults, $2.50 children 5-11, under 5 free.

Description: Life-like scenes and good graphics explaining
them with emphasis on Lancaster County. One scene depicts
the day (Sept. 27, 1777) when Lancaster was capital of the
United States. Watch for Franklin, Lincoln, Washington,
Daniel Boone. Simulated barn-raising near end of tour is
especially fun—look for tired workman near Davy Crockett.

Time Needed: 1 hour.

Tours/Programs: Audio tour available.

Codes: ♿ ☂

North Museum of Franklin and Marshall College

College and Buchanan Street, PO Box 3003
Lancaster, PA 17604-3003
(717) 291-3941

Hours: Wednesday-Saturday 9 AM-5 PM, Sunday 1:30-5 PM.
Discovery Room: Saturday and Sunday 1:30-4:30 PM.

Cost: Free.

Description: Small natural history museum with collections of skeletons, Indian artifacts, birds and mammals. Discovery Room, open for children on weekends, includes live animals, stones and bones. Planetarium Show (2:00 and 3:00 on Saturdays, 3:00 on Sundays) changes periodically.

Time Needed: 2 hours.

Tours/Programs: Many special programs throughout the year.

Codes: 👤 ⛱ 🚐

Pennsylvania Farm Museum of Landis Valley

2451 Kissel Hill Road
Lancaster, PA 17601
(717) 569-0401

Hours: Tuesday-Saturday 9 AM-5 PM, Sunday 12 Noon-5 PM.
Closed major holidays.

Cost: $3.00 adults, $1.50 children 6-17, under 6 free.

Description: Fantastic collection of buildings with 22 exhibit areas put together to demonstrate the traditional way of life in rural Pennsylvania. Tour goes through some buildings, others you explore on your own. See old wagons, fire-fighting equipment, tin and pottery shops, country store-as-it-was, and many farming tools.

Time Needed: Minimum 1 hour.

Tours/Programs: 1 hour guided tour.

Eating: Picnic areas. Inn restaurant open May-October.

Codes: ♿ 🚐

People's Place

Route 340
Intercourse, PA 17534
(717) 768-7171

Hours: April-October, Monday-Saturday 9:30 AM-9:30 PM;
November-March, Monday-Saturday 9:30 AM-4:30 PM.

Cost: $2.50 adults, $1.25 children 7-12, 6 and under free.
Separate admission fee for films.

Description: Activities just for children include the
Feeling Box, barn-raising book, energy quiz and dress-up
room. Two films run continuously: *Who Are the Amish* (25
minutes) and *Hazel's People,* (a full-length feature film)
from April through October.

Phillips Lancaster County Swiss Cheese Company

433 Centerville Road
Gordonville, PA 17529
(717) 354-4424

Hours: Monday-Friday 8 AM-5 PM, Saturday 9 AM-3 PM.
Closed Saturday in January, February and March. Closed
holidays.

Cost: Free.

Description: See a 12-minute video on how they make
cheese, then walk through small production area where
equipment is set up as if to make cheese.

Time Needed: 30-45 minutes.

Codes: 🐎

Plain and Fancy Farm

Route 340
Bird-in-Hand, PA 17505
(717) 768-8281

Hours: Monday-Saturday 11:30 AM-8 PM. Closed Christmas.

Cost: $1.00 adults for Amish House Tour and Doll Museum.

Description: Pearl's House-of-Dolls Museum holds more than
450 dolls, some as many as 150 years old. Toy shop includes
dolls made by local craftspeople. Family style restaurant and
stores.

Codes: 🐎

Railroad Museum of Pennsylvania

Route 741, Box 15
Strasburg, PA 17579
(717) 687-8628

Hours: Monday-Saturday 8:30 AM-4:30 PM, Sunday 12 Noon-4:30 PM. Open ½ hour longer when on Daylight Savings Time.

Cost: Donations requested: $1.00 adults, $.50 children.

Description: Brave visitors can walk under a 62-ton locomotive. Tremendous collection of glorious old rail cars (Pullman cars and private state rooms included) along with railroad memorabilia from conductors hats to fancy dining china. Combine with a trip across the street to ride on the Strasburg railroad!

Time Needed: 1 hour.

Eating: None, but the Strasburg Railroad across the street has picnic area and restaurant.

Codes: ♿ ✝ 🚐

Rock Ford Plantation and Kauffman Museum

881 Rock Ford Road, P.O. Box 264
Lancaster, PA 17603
(717) 392-7223

Hours: April-November, Tuesday-Saturday 10 AM-4PM, Sunday 12 Noon-4 PM.

Cost: $2.50 adults, $1.25 children 6-11.

Description: Authentically restored house and barn, with plans to restore the wood shed, ice house, smoke house and spring house. Museum has lovely collection of domestic handicrafts and decorative arts from 18th- and 19th-century southeastern Pennsylvania, including fraktur, woodcarvings, and metal work.

Time Needed: 1-2 hours.

Eating: Many picnic areas in surrounding park.

Codes: ✝ 🚐 ⚲

New Jersey was once two
states: East New Jersey
and West New Jersey.

Rough and Tumble Engineer's Museum

Box 9, Route 30
Kinzers, PA 17535
(717) 442-4249

Hours: May-October, daily 10 AM-4 PM.

Cost: $1.00 adults, children under 12 free.

Description: Equipment ranges from old household appliances to steam engines. See the massive farm equipment in motion during the exciting Annual Thresherman's Reunion in August.

Codes: 👍 ♈ ꙮ

Strasburg Railroad

See Train Rides, page 145.

Sturgis Pretzel House

219 East Main Street
Lititz, PA 17543
(717) 626-4354

Hours: Monday-Saturday 9 AM-5 PM.

Cost: $.75 adults, $.50 children.

Description: Allow plenty of time to visit—this is great fun! Hear how the early pretzel makers earned 2 cents for every 100 pretzels they made, then try twisting the dough yourself. Watch modern machines produce at the rate of 5 TONS of pretzels an hour. See soft pretzels made and cooked in the original ovens. Your admission ticket is a pretzel!

Time Needed: 1 hour (including 20-30 minute tour).

Codes: ♈

Toy Train Museum

P.O. Box 248
Strasburg, PA 17579
(717) 687-8976

Hours: May-October, and December 26-31, daily 10 AM-5 PM; April, November, early December, weekends 10 AM-5 PM.

Cost: $3.00 adults, $.75 children 7-12.

Description: The Train Collectors Association has assembled a collection of toy tinplate trains, some on shelves, some in action. Movie and collectors' information available.

Codes: 👍 ♈

Watch and Clock Museum of the NAWCC

514 Poplar Street
Columbia, PA 17512
(717) 684-8261

Hours: Tuesday-Saturday 9 AM-4 PM.

Cost: $1.50 adults, $1.25 senior citizens, $.50 children 6-17, under 6 free.

Description: Timepieces from the earliest mechanical contraption to the sophisticated "atomic clock" and related tools from around the world. See pocket sundials to moonphase wristwatches.

Time Needed: 1-1½ hours.

Codes: ♿ 👕 🚐 ⚜

Weavertown One-Room Schoolhouse

Old Philadelphia Pike (Route 340)
Bird-in-Hand, PA
(717) 768-3976

Hours: Easter-Thanksgiving, daily 10 AM-5 PM.

Cost: $1.75 adults, $1.25 children 4-11.

Description: Life-size animated figures, in a 15-minute show, depict education in a one-room schoolhouse. Real classes took place as recently as 1969; now they're all dummies.

Codes: 👕 🚐

Wheatland

1120 Marietta Avenue, Route 23
Lancaster, PA 17603
(717) 392-8721

Hours: April-November, daily 10 AM-4:15 PM. Closed Thanksgiving. Candlelight tours in early December.

Cost: $3.50 adults, $2.50 students, $1.50 under 12.

Description: Eight-minute videotape introduces visitors to home of President James Buchanan. Well-informed guides in period costume add to the atmosphere. Children's tour available for this well preserved mid-18th-century house.

Eating: Snack bar.

Codes: 🚐 ⚜

Working World

Children's curiosity about the Working World turns any behind-the-scenes visit into an instant adventure. It's easy to take children behind the counter at your local post office, behind the counter of a branch bank, behind the counter of your favorite ice cream store. The people at most workplaces are pleased to take a few minutes to explain their system to eager young listeners.

The organizations listed in this section offer official tours of varying lengths, but there are dozens of unlisted opportunities in every community. And don't forget to take the children to see your own places of work. It's important that youngsters be able to visualize where you are when you're not with them.

Ashland's Pioneer Tunnel Coal Mine and Steam Locomotive

19th and Oak Streets
Ashland, PA 17912
(717) 875-3850

Hours: May, September, October, Saturday-Sunday 10 AM-5:30 PM; Memorial Day to Labor Day, daily 10 AM-5:30 PM.

Cost: Tunnel tour: $3.50 adults, $1.50 ages 4-12, under 4 free. Locomotive: $1.50 adults, $.75 ages 4-12, under 4 free.

Description: Restored coal mine lets you see how it operated. Be sure to bring a jacket for the cold ride in an underground miner's car. Once inside the tunnel, you can get out while real coal miner guides explain the process.

Steam locomotive ride goes ¾ way around Mahonoy Mountain to a strip mine. Playground equipment next to tunnel. Anthracite Museum of Ashland nearby. Find your own fossils on the Fossil Site tour, arranged through Tunnel Office.

Time Needed: 1½-2 hours.

Eating: Food stand and picnic tables near playground.

Driving: I-76 (Schuylkill Expressway) to Rte. 202 south to 422 west. Go through Pottstown, take Reading By-Pass to Rte. 61 north. Follow to Ashland.

Codes: ♿ 🍴 🚙

Chinatown

Between 8th and 11th Streets, Vine and Arch Streets
Philadelphia, PA 19107
(215) 923-6767 (Chinese Cultural Center)

City Hall

Broad and Market Streets
Philadelphia, PA 19107
(215) 567-4476

Hours: Tour: Monday-Friday 12:30 to 1:30 PM.
Group tours: 10:30 AM, by appointment only.

Cost: Free.

Description: The only City Hall that cars can drive right
through! From William Penn's statue standing on top to the
elaborate ornamentation everywhere else, this is a visual picnic for a child. Plenty to see, including the ever-present police
escorting accused criminals. A tour includes the Mayor's
Reception Room, City Council Chambers and Caucus Room,
Conversation Hall and Court Rooms.

Codes: 👤✝️ 🚐

Fabric Workshop

1133 Arch Street, 5th and 7th floors
Philadelphia, PA 19107
(215) 568-0858

Hours: Monday-Friday 9 AM-5 PM, Saturday 12 Noon-4 PM.
Closed August.

Cost: Free.

Description: Older students of textile art enjoy talking to
artists at work and watching fabric being printed. Gallery on
7th floor.

Fire Stations

Local fire stations usually welcome young visitors, let them try
on coats and helmets, climb on the engine, and clang the bell.
Recommend parents call in advance of visit. Check local media
for events planned around October Fire Prevention Week.

When in Philadelphia, watch for Seward
Johnson's statues at 18th Street and Ben
Franklin Parkway, in front of the Four
Seasons Hotel.

Free Library of Philadelphia

Logan Square
Philadelphia, PA 19103
(215) 686-5322

Hours: Monday-Wednesday 9 AM-9 PM, Thursday-Friday
9 AM-6 PM, Saturday 9 AM-5 PM, Sunday 1 PM-5 PM.

Cost: Free.

Description: Philadelphia's largest collection of books for
children and for those studying children's literature. Also
records, tapes, magazines, foreign language books, Story Hour
Vacation Reading Clubs, and free Sunday afternoon children's
movies. Call the number above to get a free guide to branch
and regional libraries throughout Philadelphia.

HANDICAPPED SERVICES: Volunteers take reading material
to homebound readers, by appointment: call 686-5410.

Codes: 👤 🕊 🚐

General Post Office

30th and Market Streets
Philadelphia, PA 19104-9641
(215) 596-5333

Hours: Tours, Tuesday-Thursday 10 AM.

Cost: Free.

Description: Detailed one-hour tour for ages 12 and up. See
machinery, equipment and lots of behind-the-scenes details.
Requests for tours must be made in writing to Office of the
Commissioner, Room 209, General Post Office, Philadelphia,
PA 19104-9641.

Children under 12 years old are encouraged to visit their *local*
post office.

Time Needed: 1 hour.

Codes: 👤 🕊 🚐

Head House Square and New Market

2nd Street between Pine and Lombard Streets
Philadelphia, PA 19106

Description: Renovated Old Philadelphia market place. Busy
in summer with many scheduled fairs and activities for all
ages.

Herr's Snack Factory

Routes 131 and 272
Nottingham, PA 19362
(800) 523-5030

Hours: Monday-Thursday 9 AM-2 PM.

Cost: Free.

Description: One-hour tour takes you through the complete
process of making potato chips, pretzels and other snacks,
from raw materials to finished products. No more than ten
people allowed on each tour, so it's best to call ahead for
reservations.

Time Needed: 1 hour.

Eating: Free snack samples.

Driving: I-95 south to 322 west to Rte.1 south to Nottingham
Exit. Turn left off ramp, go ¼ mile. Herr's is on the right.

Codes: ☂ 🚐

Italian Market

9th Street, from Wharton to Christian Streets
Philadelphia, PA 19107

Busy neighborhood bazaar packed with *everything* for sale.

KYW-TV

Independence Mall East
5th and Market Streets
Philadelphia, PA 19104
(215) 238-4772

Hours: Monday-Friday 9 AM-5 PM.

Cost: Free.

Description: If you call several days in advance, you can
have a 45-minute tour of the television station, including stu-
dios, controls rooms, weather station and newsrooms.

Codes: ♿ ☂ 🚐

Libraries

Your local library has programs for youngsters, movies, story hours and vacation reading clubs to stimulate children's interest (*see* Free Library of Philadelphia, above). Most librarians welcome school groups.

Library for the Blind and Physically Handicapped

919 Walnut Street
Philadelphia, PA 19106
(215) 925-3213

Description: Mail order service offers large collection of large-print books, talking books, cassette books, braille books and periodicals.

Codes: 👤 🛩 🚐

Limerick Atomic Information Center

298 Longview Road
Limerick, PA 19468
(215) 495-6767

Hours: Wednesday-Sunday 10 AM-5 PM.

Cost: Free.

Description: Dinosaur footprints were discovered when they started Philadelphia Electric Company's Limerick Generating Station, and they're the first thing you see when you enter the Visitor's Center. Push-button displays and computer games explain how the station works in detail. Older children can grasp the details, younger children like the lights and graphics. Two short movies shown regularly for children ages 2-5 and 6-12 on general safety with electricity. Comic book handouts.

Time Needed: 45 minutes.

Tours/Programs: Many good programs for schools and scouts.

Driving: Take I-76 (Schuylkill Expressway) west to Rte. 202 south to Rte. 422 west to Linfield/Limerick Exit. Go left towards Linfield. Take first right onto Linfield Road, go right on Church Road, which turns into Long View Road. Follow signs.

Codes: 👤 🛩 🚐

Masonic Temple

1 North Broad Street
Philadelphia, PA 19107
(215) 988-1917

Hours: Guided tours, Monday-Friday 10 AM, 11 AM, 1 PM,
2 PM, 3 PM, Saturdays 10 AM, 11 AM. Closed Saturdays July
and August.

Cost: Free.

Description: The Masonic Temple is to Philadelphia what the
Empire State Building is to New York City: local residents keep
walking around it, instead of going in. Masons meet here every
night, and during the day the building is open for public
tours.

Anyone with a concept of world history loves this Disneyland
of architecture. Seven huge Lodge Halls inside represent seven
different ages and architectural styles. Egyptian Hall took 12
years to create and is packed with hieroglyphics and easily
recognizable symbols. Gothic Hall was built to duplicate Can-
terbury Cathedral with its medieval trappings. Etc., etc.!

Clever use of lighting simulates daylight outside each Hall
(this was the first building in Philadelphia to have electricity).
Masonic versatility uses pine to create marble-looking statues,
cast-iron stairway, plaster to resemble wood.

Time Needed: 1 hour.

Codes: ♿ ✈ 🚐

Old Masonic Lodge Building

South Willow and Lafayette Streets
Trenton, NJ 08608
(609) 393-2006

Ben Franklin and George Washington
were both Masons.

Moravian Pottery and Tile Works

Swamp Road (Route 313)
Doylestown, PA 18901
(215) 345-6722

Hours: Monday-Sunday 10 AM-5 PM. Closed January, February, Thanksgiving, Christmas, and Easter.

Cost: $2.00 adults, $1.00 students, $4.50 family.

Description: 15-minute slide show, then self-guided tour. Watch tiles being made almost exactly as they were in 1900. Be sure to see Mercer Museum (page 64) and Fonthill (page 60) while in the area.

Time Needed: 30-45 minutes.

Driving: I-95 to Willow Grove Exit 27, Rte. 611 north to Doylestown. Go right on East Court Street, past Fonthill, then left on Swamp Road. Driveway on the left.

Codes: 🦌 🚙

Newspapers

Local publications usually are pleased to give tours to groups that call ahead for reservations. Please do not call the Philadelphia newspapers.

Philadelphia International Airport

Third Floor, Terminal B, Philadelphia Airport
Philadelphia, PA 19153
(215) 492-3158

Hours: Monday-Saturday 10 AM-12 Noon.

Cost: Free.

Description: Get a tour of the operation of the entire airport, from ticketing to security checks to baggage handling. Possible to get a tour of the airfield on specially marked bus.

Time Needed: 1 hour.

Tours/Programs: School groups 3rd grade and up welcome.

Eating: Plenty throughout airport.

Codes: ♿ 🦌 🚙

Philadelphia Naval Base

Broad Street and Delaware River
Philadelphia, PA 19112
(215) 897-8775

Hours: Tours Friday and Saturday, 9 AM and 11 AM.

Cost: Free.

Description: Must be at least 8 years old and a U.S. Citizen. Bus tour includes historical sights on base, ships and mothball fleet. Reservations required, call ahead.

Time Needed: 1 hour, 15 minutes.

Codes: 🛥

Phillips Lancaster County Swiss Cheese Company

See Lancaster, page 178.

Police Stations

With advance notice, most local police stations welcome young visitors. One group of youngsters we know got a tour of their local station, toy badges, bicycle safety stickers and rules, and a humbling chance to "be in jail."

Reading Terminal Market

12th Street, from Market to Arch Streets
Philadelphia, PA 19107
(215) 922-2317, for market information
(215) 925-0948, for tour information

Description: Our country's only surviving single-span train shed is nearing 100 years old. No more trains but every imaginable kind of food. Children love to get ice cream then wander around looking at whole fish, poultry and area specialties.

Sturgis Pretzel House

See Lancaster, page 180.

Train Stations

From the Philadelphia's giant 30th Street Station to the smallest local station, the fascination still holds for children. Most are content to just wander around, but for those who want to know more, ask the station master to explain how the system works. For tours of 30th Street Station, call (215) 895-7121.

U.S. Courthouse

601 Market Street
Philadelphia, PA 19106
(215) 597-9368

Hours: Monday-Friday 10 AM-4 PM, by reservation only.

Description: Sit in the gallery and see how a real trial works. This is not just "People's Court," so call ahead and let them help you pick a trial appropriate for your child's age and understanding. If you come with a school group, the judge may come over and talk to you at break time.

Eating: Snack bar; cafeteria in Federal Building next door.

Codes: 🏃 🚶 🚙

U.S. Mint

5th and Arch Streets
Philadelphia, PA 19106
(215) 597-7350

Hours: January-March, Monday-Friday 9 AM-4:30 PM; April, October-December, Monday-Saturday 9 AM-4:30 PM; May-September, Monday-Sunday 9 AM-4:30 PM.

Cost: Free.

Description: George Washington saw the need for a national system of coins, and he started the first mint just a few blocks from here. This is Philadelphia's fourth Mint building. Free brochure explains the exhibits as you go along. First part of building open to the public shows the history of coinage, second part lets visitors watch pieces of blank metal turn into coins.

Time Needed: 1 hour.

Eating: None, but plenty of street vendors outside.

Codes: 🏃 🚶 🚙

U.S. Naval Station

c/o Public Affairs Office, Route 611
Willow Grove, PA 19090
(215) 443-1776

Hours: Tours, Thursday and Friday mornings, 10 AM.

Cost: Free.

Description: Group tours of 10-35 people go on aircraft squadron tours. If you have fewer people in your group, they let you join another group. See how a plane or helicopter squadron works, climb inside an aircraft, visit the radar control tower and weather office. Suggest reservations about 6 weeks in advance.

Time Needed: Tour lasts 2½ to 3 hours.

Eating: Option to eat in the commissary: $1.55 over 12; $.85 under age 12.

Driving: PA Turnpike to Willow Grove Exit 27. Facility is four miles north on Rte. 611.

Codes: 🚻 🚐

WCAU-TV

City Avenue and Monument Avenue
Philadelphia, PA 19131
(215) 668-5793

Hours: Monday-Friday 9 AM-5 PM.

Cost: Free.

Description: If you make a reservation several days in advance, you can have a one-hour tour of all aspects of local television, including news, weather, control rooms, etc. Maybe catch a glimpse of your favorite newsperson.

Codes: ♿ 🚻 🚐

HELPFUL PHONE NUMBERS

Emergency and Health:

Ambulance, Fire, Police, dial 911
Big Brothers/Big Sisters, (215) 668-9833 or 436-4275
Child Abuse Helpline, (215) 831-8877
Children's Emergency Shelter, (215) 686-9698
Drug and Alcohol Abuse, (215) 592-5451
Family Service Crisis Line, (215) 686-5671
Health Hotline, (800) 692-7254
Missing Children Hotline, (800) 843-5678
Poison Control Center, (215) 922-5523   or 386-2100
Runaway Hotline, (800) 231-6946
TEL-MED, (215) 829-5500
Toy Safety Hotline, (800) 638-CPSC

Pediatric Hospitals:

Alfred I. DuPont Institute
Wilmington, DE
(302) 651-4000

Child Guidance Clinic
Philadelphia, PA
(215) 243-2600

Children's Hospital of Philadelphia
Philadelphia, PA
(215) 596-9100

Children's Rehabilitation Hospital
Philadelphia, PA
(215) 877-7708

Cooper Hospital
Camden, NJ
(609) 342-2000

St. Christopher's Hospital for Children
Philadelphia, PA
(215) 427-5000

Seashore House
Philadelphia, PA
(215) 596-9103

Shriner's Hospital
Philadelphia, PA
(215) 332-4500

Tourist Phone Numbers

Philadelphia:
Independence National Historical Park Visitor Center,
(215) 597-8974 or 627-1776
International Visitors Center, (215) 823-7261
Philadelphia Visitors Center, (215) 636-1666
Philly Fun Line, (215) 568-7255
Time, (215) 846-1212
Transportation:
AMTRAK Transportation Information, (215) 824-1600
PATCO High Speed Line, (215) 922-4600
SEPTA Transportation Information, (215) 574-7800
Dial-A-Schedule (sent by mail), (215) 574-7777
Traveler's Aid Society, (215) 546-0571
Weather, (215) WE6-1212

State and County Tourist Information Numbers:

Delaware: 1-800-441-8846
New Castle County, 1-800-422-1181

New Jersey: (609) 292-2470
Burlington County, (609) 265-5068
Camden County, (609) 757-6713
Cumberland County, (609) 451-4802
Gloucester County, (609) 845-3628
Mercer County, (609) 989-6701
Salem County, (609) 935-7510, ext.202

Pennsylvania: 1-800-A-FRIEND
Berks County, (215) 375-4085
Brandywine Valley, 1-800-422-1181
Bucks County, (215) 345-4552
Chester County, (215) 431-6365
Delaware County, (215) 565-3679
Lancaster County, (717) 299-8901
Lehigh County, (215) 432-0181
Montgomery County, (215) 278-3558
Philadelphia County, (215) 636-1666
Valley Forge Fun Line, (215) 275-4636

FIRST-CHOICE ACTIVITIES

These are specially recommended by our own children:

In Delaware:

New Castle — Delaware Museum of Natural History
George Read II House and Garden

In New Jersey:

Burlington — Canoeing in the Pine Barrens
PAWS

Cumberland — Historic Bridgeton
Wheaton Village

Mercer — New Jersey State Museum

In Pennsylvania:

Berks County — Crystal Cave
Daniel Boone Homestead

Bucks County — Mercer Mile (Fonthill Museum, Mercer
Museum, Moravian Pottery and Tile Works)
Quarry Valley Farm
Sesame Place
Washington Crossing/Bowman's Hill

Chester — Hopewell Furnace and Village
Longwood Gardens
Nature Center of Charlestown

Dauphin — Hershey attractions

Delaware — Brandywine Battlefield State Park
Colonial Pennsylvania Plantation

Lancaster — Amish Homestead
Gast Classic Motor Cars Exhibit
National Wax Museum
Pennsylvania Farm Museum of Landis Valley
Strasburg Railroad and Railroad Museums
Sturgis Pretzel House
Weavertown One-Room Schoolhouse

Lehigh — Allentown Art Museum

Montgomery — Bryn Athyn/Glencairn Museum
Limerick Atomic Information Center
Valley Forge National Historic Park

Philadelphia — Independence National Historical Park
Masonic Temple
Philadelphia Zoo
Please Touch Museum
Schuylkill Valley Nature Center

DESPERATE DAYS

Birthday Party Places

Academy of Natural Sciences
Allentown Art Museum
Clover Leaf Acres
Elmwood Park Zoo
Hershey
Philadelphia Zoo
Please Touch Museum
Quarry Valley Farm
Riverbend Environmental Education Center
Roller Skating Rinks
Smith Memorial Playgrounds and Playhouses

Rainy Day Places to Visit

Ashland Pioneer Tunnel Coal Mine
Bowling
Crystal Cave
Fairmount Park Houses
Germantown houses
Historical Societies
Horticulture Center
Homesteads and Villages (see History, page 44)*
Ice/Roller skating rinks
Japanese House
Longwood Gardens *
Museums (all)
Nature Centers *
New Jersey State Aquarium
Performing Arts
Philadelphia Zoo *
Planetariums
Valley Forge National Historical Park (Visitor's Center / Film)
Working World (all)

* Some outdoor walking, from building to building, is required.

Regularly Scheduled Weekend Movies

Fall, Winter and Spring:
Academy of Natural Sciences
Bowman's Hill Wildflower Preserve
Free Library of Philadelphia and local libraries
New Jersey State Museum
PAWS Wildlife Sanctuary
Please Touch Museum
University Museum

CALENDAR OF SPECIAL EVENTS

All phone numbers listed in this section are within the Philadelphia area code (215) unless otherwise indicated. Area code (717) serves the rest of eastern Pennsylvania, (609) serves southern New Jersey; (302) serves Delaware. Long distance calls within your area code require dialing '1' before the number; your operator will remind you.

January

Ben Franklin Birthday Celebration, Franklin Institute, 448-1200.
Edgar Allan Poe's Birthday Celebration, Poe House, 597-8780.
Horseshoeing, Howell Living History Farm, (609) 737-3299.
Ice Fishing Clinic, Struble Lake, Downington, 431-6415.
Ice skating, Howell Living History Farm, (609) 737-3299.
Martin Luther King, Jr. Day, Please Touch Museum, 963-0666.
Mummers New Years Day Parade, Philadelphia. Check local media for time or call Mummer's Museum, 336-3050.
Philadelphia Auto Show, Philadelphia Civic Center, 823-7206.
Philadelphia Sport and Recreational Vehicle Show, Philadelphia Civic Center, 823-7206.
Sled Day, Howell Living History Farm, (609) 737-3299.
Storytelling, Howell Living History Farm, (609) 737-3299.
Tu B'Shvat (January or February), Morris Arboretum, 247-5777.
US Pro Indoor Tennis Championships, Spectrum, 336-3600.
Welcome Spring, Longwood Gardens, 388-6741.
Winter Nature Walk, Howell Living History Farm, (609) 737-3299.

February

Ben Franklin's Birthday, Franklin Court, 597-8974.
Ben Franklin's Birthday, Franklin Institute, 448-1200.
Black History Month, Afro-American Historical and Cultural Museum, 574-3670.
Black History Month Events, Please Touch Museum, 963-0666.
Children's Winter Craft Workshop, Howell Living History Farm, (609) 397-0449.
Chinese New Year, Chinatown, Philadelphia, 923-6767.
Chocolate Festival, Hershey, (717) 534-3900.
Dental Health Weekend, Please Touch Museum, 963-0666.
Gingerbread Day, Thompson-Neely House at Washington Crossing State Park, 493-4076.
Ice Harvest, Howell Living History Farm, (609) 737-3299.
Maple Sugar Festival, Andorra Natural Area, 242-5610.
Maple Sugar Festival, Tyler Arboretum, 566-9133.
Mummers String Band Show of Shows, Mummers Association, 356-2996.
Philadelphia Boat Show, Philadelphia Civic Center, 823-7206.
Philadelphia Home Show, Philadelphia Civic Center, 823-7206.
Presidents Day Celebration, Please Touch Museum, 963-0666.
Reading Together Celebration, Please Touch Museum, 963-0666.

Saint Valentine's Day Celebration, Philadelphia Zoo, 243-1100.
Sugar Tree Tapping, Howell Living History Farm, (609) 737-3299.
Valentine's Day Celebration, Philadelphia Museum of Art, 763-8100.
Washington's Birthday Celebrations, Valley Forge Park, 783-1077.
Welcome Spring, Longwood Gardens, 388-6741.

March

Annual Poetry Festival, statewide, coordinated by American Poetry
   Center, more than 50 events for children, (800) 546-1510.
Charter Day, Ephrata Cloisters, (717) 733-6600.
Charter Day, Pennsbury Manor, 964-0400.
Earth Science Gem and Mineral Show, Brandywine Terrace,
   Claymont, DE (302) 994-6165.
Harlem Globetrotters, Spectrum, 336-3600.
Ice Capades, Spectrum, 336-3600.
Jabberwocky, Please Touch Museum, 963-0666.
Maple Sugar Festival, Hibernia Park, 384-0290.
Maple Sugar Festival, Howell Living History Farm, (609) 737-3299.
Philadelphia Custom Car, Van and Cycle Show, Philadelphia Civic
   Center, 823-7206.
Philadelphia Flower Show, Philadelphia Civic Center, for information
   call 625-8250.
Poetry Reading Special Events, Please Touch Museum, 963-0666.
Saint Patrick's Day Celebration, Philadelphia Zoo, 243-1100.
Saint Patrick's Day Parade (check local media for times).
Sports and RV Show, Lancaster, (717) 393-7687.
Welcome Spring, Longwood Gardens, 388-6741.
Women's History Month, Please Touch Museum, 963-0666.

April

Annual Northbrook Canoe Challenge, Mortonville, 793-2279.
Arbor Day, Howell Living History Farm, (609) 737-3299.
Arbor Week, Morris Arboretum, 247-5777.
Bucks County Classic Craft Fair, Bucks County, 345-4552.
Bucks Fever Festival, Bucks County, 345-4552.
Civil War Re-enactment, Colonial Pennsylvania Plantation, 353-1777.
Dogwood Blossom Specials, W and W Railroad, Wilmington,
   (302) 998-1930.
Dogwood Blossom Time, Valley Forge Park, 783-1077.
Easter Conservatory Display, Longwood Gardens, 388-6741.
Easter Egg Hunt, Quarry Valley Farm, 794-5882.
Hagley Irish Festival, Hagley Museum, (302) 658-2400.
Historic Yellow Springs Art Show and Sale, Yellow Springs, 827-7911.
Hundred Acre Egg Hunt, Howell Living History Farm, (609) 737-3299.
Kids Volunteer Too, Please Touch Museum, 963-0666.
Kite Making and Flying, Howell Living History Farm, (609) 737-3299.
National Dance Week, 545-6344.
New Faces Day, Howell Living History Farm, (609) 737-3299.
Penn Relays, University of Pennsylvania (world's oldest and largest
   outdoor track meet), 386-0961.
Pennsylvania Crafts Fair Day, Brandywine River Museum, 388-7601.

Philadelphia Department of Recreation Table Tennis Competition, 686-0150.

Pretzel Day, Please Touch Museum, 963-0666.

Saint Waspurgis Night Festival, American Swedish Historical Museum, 389-1776.

Shad Festival and Arts and Crafts Show, Bucks County, 345-4552.

Sheep Sheering, Amish Farm and House, (717) 394-6185.

Spring Splendors Celebration, Please Touch Museum, 963-0666.

Valborgsmassoafton (traditional Swedish welcoming of spring), American Swedish Historical Museum, 389-1776.

Welcome Spring, Longwood Gardens, 388-6741.

Wissahickon Day Parade (oldest equestrian parade in Philadelphia), Fairmount Park, 247-7620.

May

A Day in Old New Castle, New Castle, (302) 322-5774.

Animals as Pets, Please Touch Museum, 963-0666.

Annual Craft Show, Colonial Pennsylvania Plantation, 353-1777.

Annual Point-to-Point Steeplechase, Winterthur Museum, (302) 888-4792 or 888-4816.

Armed Forces Weekend at Penn's Landing, Philadelphia, 923-8181.

Celebration of Old Age, Please Touch Museum, 963-0666.

Colonial Military Re-enactment, Brandywine Battlefield, 459-3342.

Devon Horse Show, Devon, 964-0550.

Fairy Tale Festival Weekend, Please Touch Museum, 963-0666.

Family Fun Day, Alfred I. DuPont Institute, Wilmington, (302) 651-6091.

Fire Expo, Dutch Wonderland, (717) 291-1888.

French Alliance Day Ceremony, Valley Forge Park, 783-7700.

Kite Festival and Contests, Morris Arboretum, 247-5777.

Kite Flying Day, Core Creek Park, 757-0571.

Manayunk Canal Day, Philadelphia, 483-7530.

Memorial Day celebrations (check local media for parades).

Memorial Day Hayrides, Howell Living History Farm, (609) 737-3299.

Mercer Folk Festival, Mercer Museum, 345-0210.

Mother's Day.

Mothers Are Special, Please Touch Museum, 963-0666.

Muppet Babies, Spectrum, 336-3600.

National Police Week (check local media for information).

Parade of Soldiers, Colonial Pennsylvania Plantation, 353-1777.

Philadelphia International Theatre Festival for Children, Annenberg Center, 898-6683.

Philadelphia Open House, Friends of Independence National Historic Park, 928-1188 (call for impressive list of events).

Plant-Your-Own Day, Howell Living History Farm, (609) 737-3299.

Radnor Spring Steeplechase Races, Malvern, 459-1900.

Rittenhouse Square Flower Market, Philadelphia, 568-6599.

Sheep Shearing, Howell Living History Farm, (609) 737-3299.

Sheep Shearing, Quarry Valley Farm, 794-5882.

Spring Honey Flow, Howell Living History Farm, (609) 737-3299.

June

Annual Crafts Fair, Delaware Art Museum, (302) 571-9590.

Annual Health Fair, for information call KYW-TV, 238-4677.

Barnum and Bailey Circus, Spectrum, 389-5000.

Buggy Day, Howell Living History Farm, (609) 737-3299.

Children's Day, W and W Railroad, Wilmington, (302) 998-1930.

Colonial Craft Day, Massey House, 356-1344.

Corestates Bike Race Championship, Ben Franklin Parkway, 629-3546.

Dairying, Howell Living History Farm, (609) 737-3299.

Delco Scottish Games and Country Fair, Devon Horse Show Grounds, Devon, 566-2898.

Departure of Continental Army, Valley Forge Park, 783-7700.

Elfreth's Alley Fete Day, Philadelphia, 568-6599.

Father's Day.

Harbor Festival at Penn's Landing, Philadelphia, 923-8181.

Head House Square Crafts Fair, Philadelphia, 568-6599.

Hog Weighing, Howell Living History Farm, (609) 737-3299.

Hopewell Passion Play, Hopewell Furnace and Village, 269-1545.

Landis Valley Fair, Pennsylvania Farm Museum of Landis Valley, (717) 569-0401.

Muster Day, Wentz Farmstead, 584-5104.

New Garden Air Show, Toughkenamon, 268-2048.

New Hope Flower Show Along the Canal, New Hope, 862-2842.

Old Newsboy's Day, Philadelphia, 568-6599.

Patriots Day, Daniel Boone Homestead, 582-4900.

Reading Air Show, Reading, 375-8551.

Rose Tree Park Summer Festival, Media, 565-7410.

Scavenger Hunt, Howell Living History Farm, (609) 737-3299.

South Jersey Woodcarver's Show and Sale, Museum of American Glass, Wheaton Village, (609) 737-3299.

State Crafts Festival at Historic Yellow Springs, 827-7911.

Teddy Bear Rally, Philadelphia Zoo, 243-1100.

July

All American Street Party, Please Touch Museum, 963-0666.

Annual Port Indian Regatta, Schuylkill River above Norristown, 666-9428.

Balloon Blast, Dutch Wonderland, (717) 291-1888.

Bastille Day, Please Touch Museum, 963-0666.

Berry Day, Howell Living History Farm, (609) 737-3299.

Children's Day, W and W Railroad, Wilmington, (302) 998-1930.

Civil War Re-enactment, Colonial Pennsylvania Plantation, 566-1725.

Farm's Birthday Party, Quarry Valley Farm, 794-5882.

Festival of Fountains, Longwood Gardens, 388-6741.

Fourth of July Celebrations, Fireworks and Parades (check local media).

Fourth of July Hayrides, Howell Living History Farm, (609) 737-3299.
Ice Cream Festival, Rockwood Museum, (302) 571-7776.
Kutztown Folk Festival, Kutztown, 683-8707.
National Tom Sawyer Day, Please Touch Museum, 963-0666.
Pennsylvania Renaissance Faire, Mt. Hope Estate and Winery,
   Cornwall (717) 665-7021.
Summer Puppet Theater Series, Springfield, 328-1200.
Warrington Lions Horse Show, Warrington, 822-0433.
Wheat Harvest, Howell Living History Farm, (609) 737-3299.
Vorspiel (Saturdays), Ephrata Cloisters, (717) 733-6600.

August

Allentown Fair, Allentown, 433-7541.
Annual Pow-Wow (gathering of United American Indians of the
   Delaware Valley), Memorial Grove, Belmont Mansion, Fairmount
   Park.
Annual Thresherman's Reunion, Rough and Tumble Engineer's
   Museum (contests, farm equipment and more), (717) 442-4249.
Antique Fire Apparatus Muster VII, Glasstown Antique Fire Brigade,
   (609) 825-6800.
August Chill, Hagley Museum, (302) 658-2400.
Bentley Brothers Circus, Devon Horse Show Grounds, for information
   call Lower Merion Police, 525-9526.
Celebration of Neighborhoods, Please Touch Museum, 963-0666.
Children's Day, W and W Railroad, Wilmington, (302) 998-1930.
Colonial Festival Day, Colonial Pennsylvania Plantation, 566-1725.
Evening Hayrides, Howell Living History Farm, (609) 737-3299.
Festival of Fountains, Longwood Gardens, 388-6741.
Goschenhoppen Folk Festival, Goschenhoppen Park, 754-6013.
Goshen Country Fair, West Chester, 692-3643.
Heritage Day, Hans Herr House, (717) 464-4438.
Hopewell Village Establishment Day, Hopewell Furnace and Village,
   582-8773.
Kids-Can-Be Day, Please Touch Museum, 963-0666.
Market Day and Festival, Quakertown, for information call 345-4552.
Middletown Grange Fair, Wrightstown, for information call 345-4552
Philadelphia Folk Festival, Old Poole Farm, Schwenksville, 247-1300.
Pennsylvania Renaissance Faire, Mt. Hope Estate and Winery,
   Cornwall, (717) 665-7021.
USTA Tennis Tournament, Spectrum, 389-5000.
Vorspiel (Saturdays), Ephrata Cloisters, (717) 733-6600.

September

American Gold Cup Equestrian Competition, Devon Horse Show
   Grounds, Devon, 964-0500.
American Music Theater Festival, Philadelphia, 988-9050.
Annual Harvest Market (weekends), Brandywine River Museum,
   388-7601.
Annual Harvest Show, Horticulture Center, Fairmount Park,
   sponsored by Pennsylvania Horticultural Society, 625-8250.

Annual Traditional Irish Music and Dance Festival, Fischer's Pool, Lansdale, 849-8899.
Antique Auto Festival, Franklin Mint Museum, 459-6168.
Blacksmithing and Horseshoeing, Howell Living History Farm, (609) 737-3299.
Chadds Ford Days and County Fair, Chadds Ford, 388-7376.
Children's Day, W and W Railroad, Wilmington, (302) 998-1930.
Corn Harvest, Howell Living History Farm, (609) 737-3299.
Ephrata Fair, Ephrata Fairgrounds, (717) 267-8773.
Fairmount Park Fall Festival, Philadelphia, 568-6599:
   Annual Juggling and Fun Skills Jubilee, 686-0053.
   Annual Schuylkill River Fishing Contest.
   Fall Festival Tennis Tournament, 686-0053.
   Fall Horse Show at Northwestern Stables, 242-0280.
   Rittenhouse Town Harvest Festival, 843-0943.
   Pennypack Fall Festival, 671-0440.
Fairy Tale Festival Weekend, Please Touch Museum, 963-0666.
Fall Festival, Hopewell Furnace and Village, 582-8773.
Germantown Founders Week, Philadelphia, 848-1777.
Grandparents' Special Day, Please Touch Museum, 963-0666.
Great Hibernia Bike Race, Hibernia Park, Coatesville, 384-0290.
Harvest Fest, Kitchen Kettle Village, (717) 768-8261.
Hero Scholarship Fund Thrill Show, JFK Stadium, 686-3400.
Honey Harvest, Howell Living History Farm, (609) 737-3299.
Ice Cream Cone Day, Please Touch Museum, 963-0666.
Kings Head of the Schuylkill Regatta, Schuylkill River by Boathouse Row, 337-9326.
Main Street Fair, Chestnut Hill Hospital, Philadelphia, 248-8200.
Penn's Landing In-water Boat Show, Philadelphia, 923-8181.
Pennsylvania Crafts Fair Day, Brandywine River Museum, 388-7601.
Pennsylvania Renaissance Faire, Mt. Hope Estate and Winery, Cornwall, (717) 665-7021.
Plowing Match, Howell Living History Farm, (609) 737-3299.
Quakertown Flight Festival, 345-4552.
Re-enactment of the Battle of Brandywine, Brandywine Battlefield State Park, 459-3342.
Sandy Flash Re-enactment, Colonial Pennsylvania Plantation, 353-1777.
Scarecrow Contest, Peddlar's Village, Lahaska, 794-7438.
Scottish Country Fair, Pipersville, 345-4552.
Von Steuben Day Parade, Philadelphia, call German Society, 627-4365.

October

Annual Harvest Market (weekends), Brandywine River Museum, 388-7601.
Annual Laerneswert, Wentz Farmstead, 584-5104.
Apple Butter Frolic, Indian Creek Farm, 723-1700.
Apple Festival, Fox Chase Farm, Philadelphia, 671-0440.
Apple Snitz Fest, Hans Herr House, (717) 464-4438.
Battle of Germantown Re-enactment, Cliveden, 848-1777.

Columbus Day Celebration, Please Touch Museum, 963-0666.
Columbus Day Parade, Philadelphia, 568-6599.
Delaware County Festival of Food, Media, 565-3679.
Fall Festival, Howell Living History Farm, (609) 737-3299.
Fire Prevention Week (check local media for events).
German-American Day, Philadelphia, 627-436.
Halloween Campfire, Brandywine Creek State Park, (302) 655-5740.
Halloween Ghost Train, W and W Railroad, Wilmington,
    (302) 998-1930.
Halloween Harvest Fest, Philadelphia Zoo, 243-1100.
Halloween Hayrides, Howell Living History Farm, (609) 737-3299.
Halloween Party, Please Touch Museum, 963-0666.
Halloween Party, Quarry Valley Farm, 794-5882.
Harvest Days, Pennsylvania Farm Museum of Landis Valley,
    (717) 569-0401.
Harvest Feast, Colonial Pennsylvania Plantation, 566-1725.
Heritage Day, Daniel Boone Homestead, 582-4900.
Historic Fallsington Day, 295-6567.
Linvilla Orchards Pumpkin Harvest and Halloween Display, 876-7116.
Pennsylvania Renaissance Faire, Mt. Hope Estate and Winery,
    Cornwall (717) 665-7021.
Pulaski Day Parade, Philadelphia, 568-6599.
Pumpkin Day and Haunted Barn, Tyler Arboretum, 566-9133.
Radnor Hunt Fall Three-Day Event, Malvern, 644-9918.
Special Needs Week, Please Touch Museum, 963-0666.
Super Sunday, Ben Franklin Parkway, Philadelphia, 299-1000.
Tales of Halloween Night, Howell Living History Farm,
    (609) 737-3299.
Wilmington Dollhouse and Miniature Show, Hotel DuPont,
    Wilmington (302) 947-6030.

November

Antique Car Club's Fun Day, Massey House, 356-1344.
Battle of Old Fort Mifflin, Philadelphia, 365-9781.
Brandywine Christmas and Train Display, Brandywine River
    Museum, 388-7601.
Chester County Farm Tours, 696-3500.
Children's Christmas Party, The Grange, (215)446-4958.
Children's Expo, Philadelphia Civic Center, 823-7206.
Christmas Display at John Wanamaker, Broad and Markets Streets,
    Philadelphia, 422-2450.
Christmas Festival at the Zoo, Philadelphia Zoo, 243-1100.
Christmas in Hershey, (717) 534-3900.
Chrysanthemum Festival, Longwood Gardens, 388-6741.
Dickens Christmas Party, Ebenezer Maxwell Mansion, 436-1861.
Disney on Ice, Spectrum, 389-5000.
Farm Day, Ashland Nature Center Barn, (302) 239-2334.
Hanukkah Festival, Philadelphia Zoo, 243-1100.
Philadelphia Dog Show, Civic Center, 823-7206.
Sesame Street Live, Philadelphia Civic Center, 823-7206.

Thanksgiving Day Parade (check local media for information).
Thanksgiving Hayrides, Howell Living History Farm, (609) 737-3299.
Victorian Christmas at Smithville, (609) 265-5068.
Wheat Threshing Bee, Howell Living History Farm, (609) 737-3299.
Winter Festival, The Grange, (215) 446-4958.
Wreath-Making Workshop, Howell Living History Farm,
   (609) 737-3299.
Yuletide Tours, Winterthur, (302) 656-8591.

December

Breakfast with Santa, John Wanamaker, Broad and Market Streets,
   Philadelphia, 422-2450.
Brian's Run, West Chester University (first Sunday in December,
   short walks and runs for all ages benefit handicapped youngsters
   injured in sports-related accidents; parents with babies in strollers,
   wheelchair athletes, thousands of youngsters participate). Call
   Larry Brandon (215) 692-5643.
Candlelight tours of most historic mansions and homesteads (call
   your favorite).
Children's Holiday Opera, Academy of Vocal Arts, Philadelphia,
   735-1685.
Christmas at Landis Valley, Pennsylvania Farm of Landis Valley,
   (717) 569-0401.
Christmas Display, Longwood Gardens, 388-6741.
Fairmount Park Houses Christmas Tours, 763-8100 ext. 266.
Flashlight Christmas Carol Concert, Franklin Institute, 448-1200.
Gingerbread Jamboree, Please Touch Museum, 963-0666.
Hanukkah Festival, Philadelphia Zoo, 243-1100.
Holiday Fest, Philadelphia Zoo, 243-1100.
Holiday Happenings, Please Touch Museum, 963-0666.
Holly Ramble, Tyler Arboretum, 566-9133.
Ice Follies, Spectrum, 389-5000.
Koziar's Christmas Village, Bernville, PA, 488-1110.
Kwanzaa, Afro-American Hist. and Cultural Museum, 574-0380.
Lucia Fest and Julmarknad, American-Swedish Historic Museum,
   389-1776.
Moravian Christmas Putz, Bethlehem, 866-5661.
Nutcracker Ballet, Academy of Music, 978-1420.
Old Fashioned Christmas, Howell Living History Farm,
   (609) 737-3299.
Re-enactment of Washington Crossing the Delaware, Washington
   Crossing State Park, 493-4076.
Re-enactment of Washington's March, Valley Forge Park, 783-1077.
Ridley Creek State Park Wassail Tour, Media, 566-4800.
Santa Claus Specials, W and W Railroad, Wilmington, (302) 999-9008.
Storybook Land Christmas Time, (609) 641-7847.
Swedish Christmas, Please Touch Museum, 963-0666.

Appendix A: Free Activities

These places do not charge an admission fee, but some (*)
request a donation to help with expenses.

Airdrie Forest Preserve
Allentown Art Museum
Anderson Bakery
Andorra Natural Area
Ashland Nature Center
Atwater Kent Museum
Awbury Arboretum
Balch Institute
Betsy Ross House
Blockson Afro-American Collection
Bowman's Hill (except Tower)
Brandywine Battlefield State Park
Briar Bush Nature Center
Brinton 1704 House *
Bucks County Covered Bridges
Camden County Environmental Center
Campbell Museum
Candy Americana Museum
Carpenters Hall
Cathedrals and Churches
Chocolate World, Hershey
Churchville Nature Center
CIGNA Museum
City Hall
Cohanzick Zoo
Congress Hall
Cool Valley Preserve
David Rittenhouse Lab Observatory
Delancey Street
Delaware Art Museum *
Delaware County Institute of Science
Drexel University Museum
Edgar Allan Poe Historic Site
Elfreth's Alley and Museum
Elmwood Park Zoo
Fabric Workshop
Fairmount Park
Fairmount Park Houses
Fairmount Park Water Works
Feed ducks at local pond
Fire stations
Fireman's Hall Museum
First Pennsylvania Bank Museum
Four Mills Nature Reserve
Franklin Court
Franklin Mint
Franklin's Bust

Free Library of Philadelphia
General Post Office
George Lorimer Nature Preserve
George Read II House and Garden
German Society of Pennsylvania
Germantown Historical Society Museum Complex
Germantown Mennonite Information Center
Graff House
Grundy Museum
Hall of Fame Sports Museum
Hawk Mountain Sanctuary
Head House Square
Historic Burlington County Prison Museum
Historic Yellow Springs *
Historical Societies
Horticulture Center *
Howell Living History Farm
Ile-Ife Museum of Afro-American History
Independence Hall
Independence National Historical Park
Independence National Historical Park Visitor Center
Institute of Contemporary Art *
Japanese House
Jenkins Arboretum
KYW-TV
Kosciuszko National Memorial
Lancaster Newspaper Newseum
La Salle University Art Museum
Laurel Hill Cemetery
Liberty Bell Pavilion *
Libraries
Limerick Atomic Information Center
Masonic Temple
Memorial Hall
Mennonite Heritage Center
Merrymead Farm
Mill Grove
Mutter Museum
Nail House Museum
National Archives
Nature Center of Charlestown
New Hall
New Jersey State Museum and Planetarium
Newcomen Library and Museum *
Newlin Grist Mill Park
Nolde Forest Environmental Education Center
North Museum
Old Barracks Museum *
Old City Hall
Old Town Hall
Paley Design Center
Parks and playgrounds

Peace Valley Nature Center
Peale House
Pemberton House
Pennsylvania Dutch Visitors Bureau
Pennsylvania Horticultural Society
Pennsylvania Hospital Physic Garden
Pennsylvania Hospital Nursing Museum
Pennypacker Mills
Philadelphia Art Alliance
Philadelphia International Airport
Philadelphia Maritime Museum and Workshop on Water
Philadelphia Naval Base
Phillips Lancaster Swiss Cheese Co.
Railroad Museum
Places of worship
Police stations
Polish-American Cultural Association
Pool Wildlife Sanctuary *
Post offices
Rancocas Nature Center
Reading Public Museum and Art Gallery *
Rickett's Circus
Rittenhousetown
Riverbend Environmental Education Center
Rodin Museum *
Ryerss Museum
Sanderson Museum *
Scott Arboretum
Second Bank of the United States
Silver Lake Nature Center
Smith Civil War Monument
Smith Memorial Playgrounds and Playhouses
Sports (most college sports)
Streitweiser Trumpet Museum
Tinicum National Environmental Center
Tourist information centers
U.S. Courthouse
U.S. Mint
U.S. Naval Station
University Museum *
Upper Schuylkill Valley Farm Park
Valley Forge National Historic Park
WCAU-TV
Wagner Free Institute of Science
Wanamaker's Organ Concerts
War Library and Museum
Walt Whitman Home
Washington Crossing State Park
Wentz Farmstead
Woodmere Art Museum *
Woodruff Indian Museum

Appendix B: Activities With Wheelchair Access

Academy of Natural Sciences
Afro-American Historical and Cultural Museum
Allentown Art Museum
Amish Farm and House
Amish Village
Arthur Ashe Youth Tennis Center (wheelchair tennis)
Ashland Nature Center
Ashland Pioneer Tunnel Coal Mine and Steam Locomotive
Atwater Kent Museum
Balch Institute
Beth Shalom Synagogue
Blockson Afro-American Collection
Boyertown Museum of Historic Vehicles
Brandywine Battlefield Park
Brandywine River Museum
Brandywine Zoo
Briar Bush Nature Center (inside only; no paved trails)
Bryn Athyn Cathedral
Buten Museum
Camden County Environmental Studies Center
Campbell Museum
Carousel House, Philadelphia Department of Recreation
Carpenters Hall (ground floor only)
Cathedrals and Churches
Churchville Nature Center (special paved trail for the handicapped)
CIGNA Museum (first floor gallery only)
City Hall
Choo-Choo Barn
Cliveden
Cohanzick Zoo
Colonial Flying Corps Museum
Colonial Pennsylvania Plantation (bumpy)
Congress Hall (ground floor only)
Daniel Boone Homestead (minimal access)
Delaware Art Museum
Delaware Museum of Natural History
Dorney Park
Drexel University Museum
Dutch Wonderland
Eagles Games
Elmwood Park Zoo (bumpy boardwalk with wheelchair/stroller gate)
Ephrata Cloisters
Fireman's Hall Museum
First Pennsylvania Bank Museum

Flyers games
Fonthill Museum (very limited)
Four Mills Nature Reserve (inside only, no paved trails)
Franklin Court
Franklin Institute
Franklin Mint
Free Library
Gast Classic Motor Cars
General Post Office
Glencairn Museum
Graff House (ground floor only)
Green Hills Farm (ground floor only)
Hagley Museum and Eleutherian Mills
Hall of Fame Sports Museum
Hans Herr House
Hershey activities
Historic Fallsington (uneven ground)
Historical Society of Pennsylvania
Hope Lodge
Hopewell Furnace and Village
Horticulture Center
Howell Living History Farm (handicapped parking in back)
Hutchinson Gym Pool (handicapped swimming)
Ile-Ife Museum of Afro-American Culture
Independence Hall (ground floor only)
Independence National Historical Park and Visitor Center
Institute of Contemporary Art
KYW-TV
Kosciuszko National Memorial (ground floor only)
La Salle University Art Museum
Liberty Bell Pavilion
Limerick Atomic Information Center
Longwood Gardens (wheelchairs available)
Mary Merritt Doll Museum
Masonic Temple
Mennonite Meeting House
Mercer Museum
Merritt's Museum of Childhood
Merrymead Farm (on grass)
Mikveh Israel Synagogue
Mill Bridge Village
Morris Arboretum (limited)
Mummers Museum
Nail House Museum
National Archives
National Museum of American Jewish History (ground floor only)
National Wax Museum
New Hall (ground floor only)
New Jersey State Aquarium

New Jersey State Museum and Planetarium
Newcomen Library and Museum (limited; a few steps)
Newlin Grist Mill Park (limited)
Nolde Environmental Education Center
Norman Rockwell Museum
North Museum
Old Barracks Museum
Old City Hall
Old Dutch House
Old Fort Mifflin (on grass)
Old Town Hall
PAWS Wildlife Sanctuary (dirt road available for access if necessary)
Paley Design Center
Peale House
Pemberton House (ground floor only)
Pennsbury Manor
Pennsylvania Academy of the Fine Arts
Pennsylvania Farm Museum of Landis Valley (somewhat restricted)
Pennsylvania Hospital Nursing Museum
Pennsylvania Hospital Physic Garden
Pennypacker Mills
Perelman Antique Toy Museum
Performing arts (most, call ahead)
Philadelphia International Airport
Philadelphia Maritime Museum
Philadelphia Museum of Art
Philadelphia Zoo
Phillies
Phillips Mushroom Museum
Places of worship (most, call ahead)
Please Touch Museum
Pool Wildlife Sanctuary (not easy)
Port of History Museum
Quarry Valley Farm (on grass)
Railroad Museum
Reading Public Museum and Art Gallery (difficult)
Rockwood
Rodin Museum
Rough and Tumble Engineer's Museum
Ryerss Museum
Schuylkill Valley Nature Center
   (highly recommended indoors and out)
Scott Arboretum
Sesame Place
'76ers games
Six Flags Great Adventure
Smithville (limited)
Smith Memorial Mansion and Playground (very little)
Sports, spectator (most, call ahead)

Sports, Active: Arthur Ashe Youth Tennis Center (wheelchair tennis)
    Carousel House, Philadelphia Department of Recreation
    Hutchinson Gym Pool (handicapped swimming)
    Springton Manor Farm (fishing from paved dock)
    Temple Rollin' Owls (wheelchair basketball team)
    Thorncroft Equestrian Center (handicapped riding)
Springton Manor Farm (fishing from paved dock)
Storybook Land
Tinicum National Environmental Center
Thorncroft Equestrian Center
Toy Train Museum
University Museum
Upper Schuylkill Valley Farm Park (on grass)
U.S. Courthouse
U.S. Mint
Valley Forge National Historic Park
WCAU-TV
Washington Crossing Historic Park (get brochure for rest-rooms)
Watch and Clock Museum
Wentz Farmstead
Wheaton Village
Wings
Winterthur
Woodruff Indian Museum

Appendix C: Activities for School Groups

These offer special programs for school groups. Advance reservations are requested.

Academy of Natural Sciences
Afro-American Historical and Cultural Museum
Airdrie Forest Preserve
Allentown Art Museum
American Swedish Historical Museum
Amish Farm and House
Amish Homestead
Amish Village
Andorra Natural Area
Ashland Nature Center
Ashland Pioneer Tunnel Coal Mine
Atwater Kent Museum
Awbury Arboretum
Balch Institute
Barclay Farmstead
Barns-Brinton House
Bartram's House and Gardens
Batsto Village
Belmont Mansion
Betsy Ross House
Blockson Afro-American Collection
Bowman's Hill Wildflower Preserve
Boyertown Museum of Vehicles
Brandywine Battlefield State Park
Brandywine River Museum
Brandywine Zoo
Briar Bush Nature Center
Brinton 1704 House
Bryn Athyn Cathedral
Buten Museum
Camden County Environmental Studies
Campbell Museum
Carpenters Hall
Cedar Grove
Chad House
Choo-Choo Barn
CIGNA Museum
City Hall
Cliveden
Cohanzick Zoo
Colonial Pennsylvania Plantation
Congress Hall
Conrad Weiser Homestead
Cool Valley Preserve
Cornwall Furnace
Crystal Cave

Daniel Boone Homestead
Delaware Art Museum
Delaware County Institute of Science
Delaware Museum of Natural History
Drexel University Museum
Elmwood Park Zoo
Ephrata Cloisters
Fire stations (most)
Fonthill Museum
Four Mills Nature Reserve
Franklin Court
Franklin Institute
Franklin Mint
Gazela
George Read II House and Garden
German Society of Pennsylvania
Germantown Historical Museum
Germantown Houses
Glencairn Museum
Graeme Park
Graff House
Green Hills Farm
Hagley Museum and Eleutherian Mills
Hawk Mountain
Herrs Snack Factory (small groups only)
Hershey: all features
Historic Fallsington
Historical Burlington Prison Museum
Historical societies
Hope Lodge
Hopewell Furnace and Village
Horticulture Center
Howell Living History Farm
Ile-Ife Museum of Afro-American Culture
Independence Hall
Independence National Historical Park
Independence National Historical Park Visitor Center
Institute of Contemporary Art
Japanese House
Kosciuszko National Memorial
La Salle University Art Museum
Laurel Hill
Lemon Hill
Liberty Bell Pavilion
Libraries (most)
Limerick Information Center
Longwood Gardens
Mary Merritt Doll Museum
Masonic Temple
Massey House
Mennonite Heritage Center

Mercer Museum
Merritt's Museum of Childhood
Merrymead Farm
Moravian Pottery and Tile Works
Morris Arboretum
Morton Homestead
Mount Pleasant
Mummers Museum
Museum of the Philadelphia Civic Center
Mutter Museum
National Archives
National Museum of American Jewish History
National Wax Museum
Nature Center of Charlestown
New Hall
New Jersey State Aquarium
New Jersey State Museum and Planetarium
Newcomen Library and Museum
Newlin Grist Mill Park
Nolde Environmental Center
Norman Rockwell Museum
North Museum
Old Barracks Museum
Old City Hall
Old Town Hall
Ormiston
PAWS Wildlife Sanctuary
Peale House
Pemberton House
Pennsbury Manor
Pennsylvania Academy of Fine Arts
Pennsylvania Dutch Visitors Bureau
Pennsylvania Farm Museum of Landis Valley
Pennypack Environmental Center
Pennypacker Mills
Perelman Antique Toy Museum
Philadelphia International Airport
Philadelphia Maritime Museum
Philadelphia Maritime Museum's Workshop on Water
Philadelphia Museum of Art
Philadelphia Zoo
Phillips Mushroom Museum
Please Touch Museum
Police stations (most)
Polish American Cultural Association
Port of History Museum
Post offices (most)
Pusey House and Landingford Plantation
Quarry Valley Farm
Rancocas Nature Center
Reading Museum and Art Gallery
Rittenhouse Lab Observatory

Riverbend Environmental Center
Rock Ford Plantation
Rockwood
Rodin Museum
Rosenbach Museum
Ryerss Museum
Sanderson Museum
Schuylkill Valley Nature Center
Scott Arboretum
Second Bank of United States
Silver Lake Nature Center
Smithville
Springton Manor Farm
Strawberry Mansion
Streitweiser Trumpet Museum
Sweetbrier
Tinicum National Environmental Center
Tyler Arboretum
University Museum
Upper Schuylkill Valley Farm Park
U.S. Courthouse
U.S. Mint
U.S. Naval Station
USS *Becuna*
USS *Olympia*
Valley Forge National Historic Park
Wagner Free Institute
Walt Whitman Home
Washington Crossing State Park
Watch and Clock Museum
Wentz Farmstead
Wharton Esherick Museum
Wheatland
Wheaton Village
Winterthur
Woodford
Woodmere Art Museum
Zoo America

Appendix D: Activities Grouped By County

Delaware

New Castle County:
Ashland Nature Center
Brandywine Creek State Park
Brandywine Zoo
Delaware Art Museum
Delaware Children's Theater
Delaware Museum of Natural History
George Read II House and Garden
Grand Opera House
Hagley Museum and Eleutherian Mills
Historic Society of Delaware
MV Lady Christina Harbor Cruises
New Castle County Parks
Old Dutch House
Old Swedes Church
Old Town Hall
Rockwood
Skating Club of Wilmington
University of Delaware
Warner Enterprises
Wilmington and Western Railroad
Winterthur

New Jersey

Atlantic County:
Storybook Land

Burlington County:
Batsto Village
Bel Haven Lake
Buttonwood Stables
Chesterfield Christmas Tree Farm
Conte Farms
Discover Adventure
Evesham Skating Center, Inc.
Fernbrook Farm Nursery
Forks Landing Marina
Four Winds Farm
Golden Wings
Haines Tree Farm
Historic Burlington County Prison Museum
Indian Acres Tree Farm
John's Corner Farm
Juliustown Christmas Tree Farm
Lucky C Stables
Mick's Canoe Rental
New Jersey Historical Society

Other Place
Paradise Lakes Campground
PAWS Wildlife Sanctuary
Pine Barrens Canoe Rental
Rancocas Nature Center
Richard T. DeCou Farm
Rolling Acres Riding School
Smithville
Train T Plantation
Wading Pines Campgrounds

Camden County:
Barclay Farmstead
Camarata Children's Theatre
Camden County Environmental Studies Center
Campbell Museum
Cherry Hill Skating Club
Clementon Amusement Park
Clover Leaf Acres
Deptford Skating Center
Lucca Tree Farms
New Jersey Historical Society
New Jersey State Aquarium
Puttin' On the Ritz Children's Theatre
Walt Whitman Center
Walt Whitman Home

Cumberland County:
Cohanzick Zoo
Hall of Fame Sports Museum
Historic Bridgeton Walking Tour
Nail House Museum
Wheaton Village
Woodruff Indian Museum

Gloucester County:
Exley's Country Lane Nursery
Glassboro Summer Theatre
Gloucester County Historical Society
Henry Banff
Holly Oak Farm
Tuck-A-Lou Orchards

Ocean County:
Six Flags Great Adventure

Mercer County:
Howell Living History Farm
Mercer County Parks
New Jersey State Historical Commission
New Jersey State Museum and Planetarium
Old Barracks Museum
Old Masonic Lodge Building
War Memorial Building

Salem County:
Appel Farm Arts
Cowtown Rodeo
Glassboro State College Summer Theatre
New Jersey Historical Society

Pennsylvania

Berks County:
Berks County Parks
Blue Mountain and Reading Railroad
Boyertown Museum of Historic Vehicles
Conrad Weiser Homestead
Cornwall Furnace
Crystal Cave
Daniel Boone Homestead
Hawk Mountain Sanctuary
Hawk Mountain Railroad Line
Mary Merritt Doll Museum
Merritt's Museum of Childhood
Nolde Environmental Education Center
Reading Public Museum and Art Gallery

Bucks County:
Appleville Orchards
Bowman's Hill Wildflower Preserve
Bucks County Balloon Adventures
Bucks County Carriages
Bucks County Covered Bridges
Bucks County Historical Society
Bucks County Parks
Bucks County Playhouse
Bucks County Tourist Commission
Churchville Nature Center
Coryell's Ferry Boat
Fonthill Museum
Ghost Tours
Grundy Museum
Historic Fallsington, Inc.
Howell Living History Farm
Indian Walk Christmas Tree Farm
Jug Hill Christmas Tree Farm
Magical Mystery Flights, Inc.
McArdle Tree Farm
Mercer Museum
Moravian Pottery and Tile Works
New Hope Information Center
New Hope Mule Barge
New Hope Steam Railway
Nonesuch Farm
Our Lady of Czestochowa
Paul Valley Farm Market
Peace Valley Nature Center

Pennsbury Manor
Pine Run Christmas Tree Farm
Point Pleasant Canoes
Quarry Valley Farm
Sesame Place
Silver Lake Nature Center
Washington Crossing State Park
Watson Tree Farm

Carbon County:
Little Gap
Mauch Chunk Lake Park

Chester County:
Airdrie Forest Preserve
At Your Service Tours
Barnards Orchards
Brandywine Bicycle Club
Brinton 1704 House
Chester County Historical Society
Chester County Parks
Children's Musical Theater at Valley Forge Music Fair
Colonial Flying Corps Museum
Cool Valley Preserve
Deer Valley Tree Farm
Duncan's Farm Market
Gateway Stables
George Lorimer Nature Preserve
Grand Slam, USA
Great Valley Stables
Herrs Snack Factory
Highland Orchards
Historic Yellow Springs
Hopewell Furnace and Village
Kimber Vu Farm
Longwood Gardens
Malickson's Christmas Tree FArm
Nature Center of Charlestown
Newcomen Library and Museum
Northbrook Canoe
Northbrook Orchards
Nussex Farms
Pusey House and Landingford Plantation
Springton Manor Farm
Streitweiser Trumpet Museum
Thorncroft Equestrian Center
Valley Forge National Historic Park
Valley Forge Park Visitor Center
West Chester and Barleysheaf Players
Wetherill Christmas Trees
Wharton Esherick Museum

Dauphin County:
Hershey attractions

Delaware County:
Barns-Brinton House
Brandywine Battlefield State Park
Brandywine River Museum
CN Skate Palace, Ltd.
Camerata Opera Theater
Chad House
Chadds Ford Equestrian Center
Chadds Peak
Colonial Pennsylvania Plantation
Delaware County Community College Theater
Delaware County Institute of Science
Delaware County Parks
Eastern College Planetarium
Franklin Mint
Grand Slam USA
Grange
Hedgerow Theatre
Linvilla Orchards
Magical Mystery Flights, Inc.
Manbecks Orchards
Marple Newtown Historical Society
Massey House
Morton Homestead
Newlin Grist Mill Park
Playhouse Theater
Radnor Historical Society
Sanderson Museum
Scott Arboretum
Skatium
Springton Manor Farm
Tyler Arboretum
Villanova University
Villanova University Theatre

Lakawana County:
Montage

Lancaster County:
Abe's Buggy Ride
Amish Country Tours/Dutchland Tours
Amish Farm and House
Amish Homestead
Amish Villages
Anderson Bakery
Candy Americana Museum
Choo-Choo Barn
Dutch Wonderland
Dutchland Tours
Ed's Buggy
Ephrata Cloisters
Folk Craft Center and Museum
Forest Ridge Stables

Fulton Opera House
Gast Classic Motor Cars Exhibit
Great Adventure Balloon Club
Hans Herr House
Historic Lancaster Walking Trail
Kitchen Kettle Village
Lancaster County Heritage Center
Lancaster County Parks
Lancaster Newspaper Newseum
Mennonite Heritage Center
Mennonite Meeting House
Mill Bridge Village
National Wax Museum
New Horizons Bike Adventures
North Museum
Pennsylvania Dutch Visitor's Bureau
Pennsylvania Farm Museum of Landis Valley
Phillips Lancaster County Swiss Cheese Co.
Plain and Fancy Farm
Railroad Museum of Pennsylvania
Rockford Plantation
Rough and Tumble Engineer's Museum
Smoketown Airport Aerial Tours
Strasburg Railroad
Sturgis Pretzel House
Toy Train Museum
Watch and Clock Museum of the NAWCC
Water Buggy
Weavertown One-Room Schoolhouse
Wheatland

Lehigh County:
Allentown Art Museum
Doe Mountain
Dorney Park and Wildwater Kingdom
Lafayette College
Lehigh County Historical Society
Lehigh County Parks
Lehigh University
Overlook Orchards
Pool Wildlife Sanctuary
Strawberry Acres

Luzerne County:
Big Boulder
Jack Frost
Split Rock

Lycoming County:
Crystal Cave Ski Center

Monroe County:
Camelback
Shawnee

Montgomery County:
Ashford Farms
Beth Shalom Synagogue
Boswell's Tree Farm
Briar Bush Nature Center
Bryn Athyn Swedenborgian Cathedral
Buten Museum
Cheltenham Playhouse Children's Theatre
Eastern College Planetarium
Elmwood Park Zoo
Four Mills Nature Reserve
Glencairn Museum
Graeme Park
Hope Lodge
Koziar's Christmas Village
Kutz's Christmas Tree Farm
Limerick Atomic Information Center
Merrymead Farm
Mill Grove
Montgomery County Historical Museum
Montgomery County Parks
Pennypacker Mills
Pine Hill Farm
Riverbend Environmental Education Center
Spring Meadow Farm
Spring Mountain
Turner Airport Aerial Tours
Upper Schuylkill Valley Farm Park
U.S. Naval Station
Valley Forge National Historic Park
Wentz Farmstead

Philadelphia County:
ABC Bus and Walking Tour
Academy Boys Choir
Academy of Natural Sciences
Aero Aviation
Afro-American Historical and Cultural Museum
Allens Lane Center
American Swedish Historical Museum
American Theater Arts for Youth
American Youth Hostels
Andorra Natural Area
Annenburg Center Theater for Children
Art Museum Shuttle
Arthur Ashe Youth Tennis Center
Atwater Kent Museum
Audio Walking Tour of Philadelphia
Awbury Arboretum
Balch Institute
Ballet des Jeunes
Bartram's House and Gardens

Belmont Mansion
Ben Franklin Carriages
Betsy Ross House
Bicycle Coalition
Black History Strolls
Blockson Afro-American Collection
Burholme Golf
Bushfire Theater
Byrne, J.F., Golf Course
Carman Roller Skating Rink
Carpenter's Hall
Cathedral Basilica of Saints Peter and Paul
Cathedral of the Immaculate Conception
Cedar Grove
Centipede Tours
Chamounix Mansion
Children's Hospital
Chinatown
Christ Church
Christmas Trolley Tours
CIGNA Museum
City Hall
Civic Center Museum
Cliveden
Cobbs Creek Golf Course
Cobbs Creek Skate House
Community Education Center
Concerto Soloists Concerts for Children
Concord School House
Congress Hall
Conwell Dance Theater
Delancey Street
Deshler-Morris House
Drexel University Museum Collection
Drexel University Sports and Theater
Eagles
Ebenezer Maxwell Mansion
Edgar Allan Poe National Historic Site
Elfreth's Alley and Museum
Elmwood Roller Skating Rink
Fabric Workshop
Fairmount Park and all attractions
Fireman's Hall Museum
First Pennsylvania Bank Museum
Fleet Helicopter
Flyers
Foundation for Architecture Tour
Franklin Court
Franklin D. Roosevelt Park
Franklin Institute and Fels Planetarium
Franklin's Bust
Free Library of Philadelphia

Free Quaker Meeting House
Gazela of Philadelphia
General Post Office of Philadelphia
German Society of Pennsylvania
Germantown
Germantown Historical Society Museum Complex
Germantown Mennonite Information Center ?
Gloria Dei Church
Graff House
Grumblethorpe
Head House Square and New Market
Historical Society of Pennsylvania
Horticulture Center
Ile-Ife Museum of Afro-American Culture
Independence Hall
Independence National Historical Park
Independence National Historical Park Visitor Center
Institute of Contemporary Art
Italian Market
Japanese House
Jenkins Arboretum
John Byrne Golf Club
John Wanamaker's Organ Concerts and Breakfast With Santa
Juniata Golf Course
Kosciuszko National Memorial
KYW-TV
La Salle University Art Museum
Laurel Hill
Laurel Hill Cemetery
Lemon Hill
Liberty Bell Pavilion
Liberty Belle Charters, Inc.
Lincoln Flying Service
Loudon
Masonic Temple
Memorial Hall
Mikveh Israel Synagogue
Morris Arboretum
Mother Bethel A.M.E. Church
Mount Pleasant
Mummers Museum
Museum Family Theater
Museum of the Philadelphia Civic Center
Mutter Museum
National Archives
National Museum of American Jewish History

New Freedom Theater
New Hall
Norman Rockwell Museum
Northeast Aviation
Old City Hall

Old First Reformed Church
Old Fort Mifflin
Old Pine Street Presbyterian Church
Ormiston
Paley Design Center
Peale House
Pemberton
Penns Landing
Pennsylvania Academy of Fine Arts
Pennsylvania Ballet Company
Pennsylvania Horticultural Society
Pennsylvania Hospital Nursing Museum
Pennsylvania Hospital Physic Garden
Pennypack Environmental Center
Perelman Antique Toy Museum
Philadelphia Art Alliance
Philadelphia Boys Choir and Chorale
Philadelphia Carriages
Philadelphia Civic Ballet Company
Philadelphia College of Textiles and Science
Philadelphia Department of Recreation
Philadelphia International Airport
Philadelphia Marionette Theater
Philadelphia Maritime Museum
Philadelphia Maritime Museum's Workshop on the Water
Philadelphia Museum of Art
Philadelphia Naval Base
Philadelphia Orchestra's Children's Concerts
Philadelphia Tours
Philadelphia Zoo
Phillies
Plays and Players Children's Theater
Please Touch Museum
Polish American Cultural Association
Public Canoe House
R & S Harbor Tours, Inc.
Reading Market
Rickett's Circus
Rittenhouse Lab Observatory
Rittenhousetown
Rizzo Rink
Rodin Museum
Roosevelt Golf Course
Rosenbach Museum and Library
Ryerss Museum
Saint Joseph's University
Saint Peter's Episcopal Church

Scanlan Recreation Center
Schuylkill Discovery
Schuylkill Valley Nature Center
Second Bank of the U.S.

Settlement Music School
'76 Carriage Company
'76ers
Simons Recreation Center
Smith Civil War Monument
Smith Memorial Playgrounds and Playhouses
Spirit of Philadelphia
Sports, Active and Spectator
Stenton
Sterling Helicopter
Strawberry Mansion
Sweetbrier Mansion
Temple University
Theater Center of Philadelphia
Tinicum National Environmental Center
Town and Country Tours
Tracey Tours/Carol Lines
University Museum
University of Pennsylvania
University of the Arts
Upsala
U.S. Courthouse
U.S. Mint
USS *Becuna*
USS *Olympia*
WCAU, WPVI, WXPN
Wagner Free Institute of Science
Walnut Lane Golf Course
Wissahickon Ice Skating Club
Wistar Institute Museum
Woodford
Woodmere Art Museum
Wyck

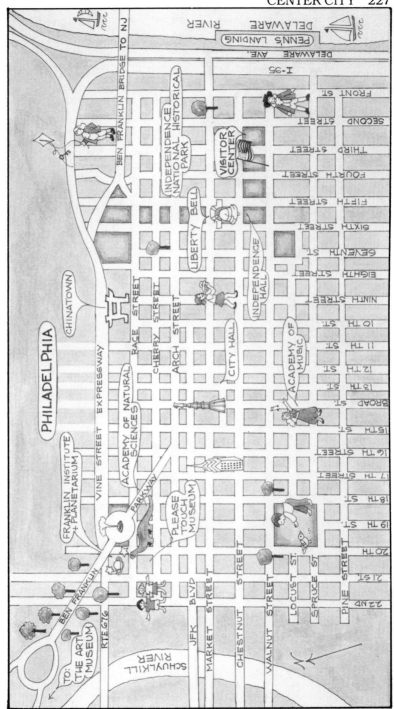

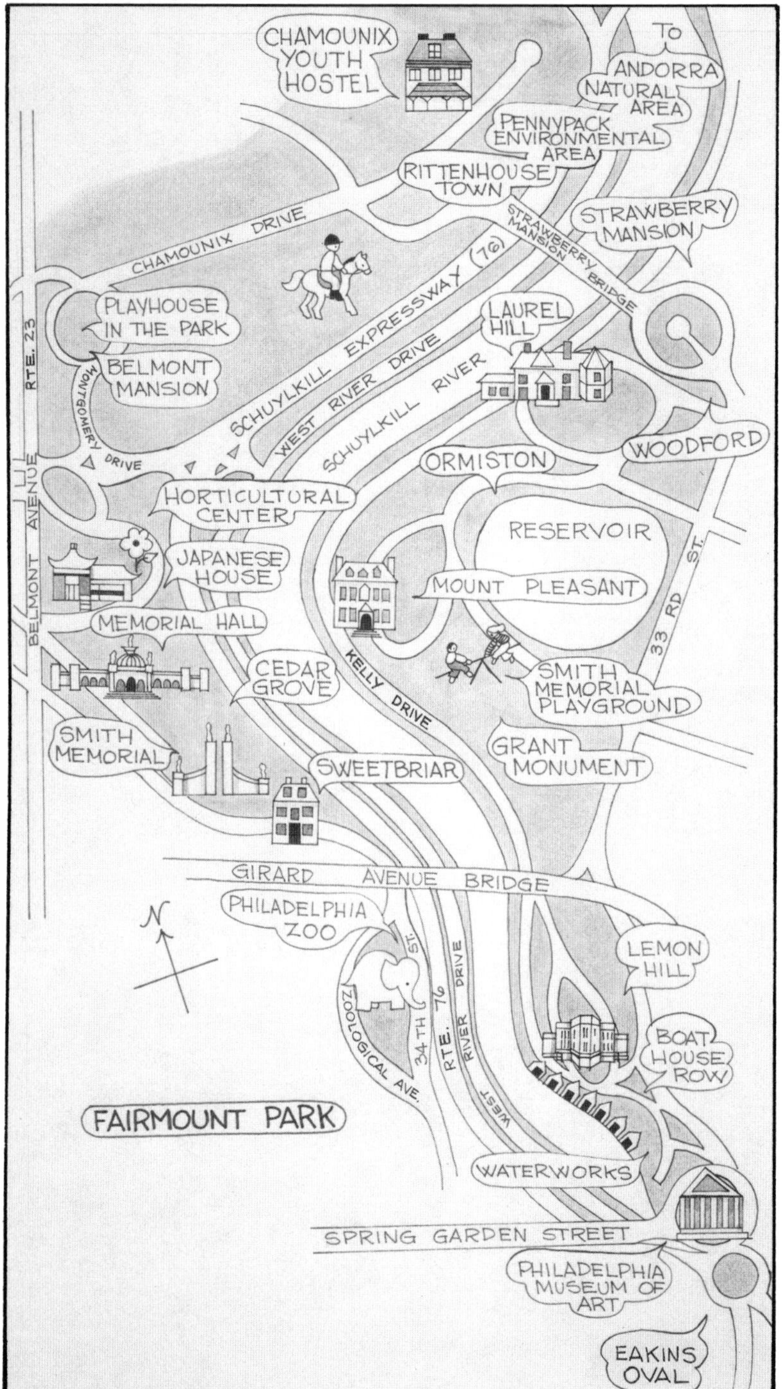
CHAMOUNIX YOUTH HOSTEL
TO ANDORRA NATURAL AREA
PENNYPACK ENVIRONMENTAL AREA
RITTENHOUSE TOWN
STRAWBERRY MANSION
CHAMOUNIX DRIVE
STRAWBERRY MANSION BRIDGE
SCHUYLKILL EXPRESSWAY (76)
PLAYHOUSE IN THE PARK
LAUREL HILL
BELMONT MANSION
RTE. 23
MONTGOMERY DRIVE
WEST RIVER DRIVE
SCHUYLKILL RIVER
WOODFORD
ORMISTON
HORTICULTURAL CENTER
RESERVOIR
BELMONT AVENUE
JAPANESE HOUSE
MOUNT PLEASANT
33 RD ST.
MEMORIAL HALL
KELLY DRIVE
CEDAR GROVE
SMITH MEMORIAL PLAYGROUND
SMITH MEMORIAL
GRANT MONUMENT
SWEETBRIAR
GIRARD AVENUE BRIDGE
PHILADELPHIA ZOO
N
LEMON HILL
34 TH ST.
RTE. 76
WEST RIVER DRIVE
ZOOLOGICAL AVE.
BOAT HOUSE ROW
FAIRMOUNT PARK
WATERWORKS
SPRING GARDEN STREET
PHILADELPHIA MUSEUM OF ART
EAKINS OVAL

GREATER PHILADELPHIA
CAMDEN

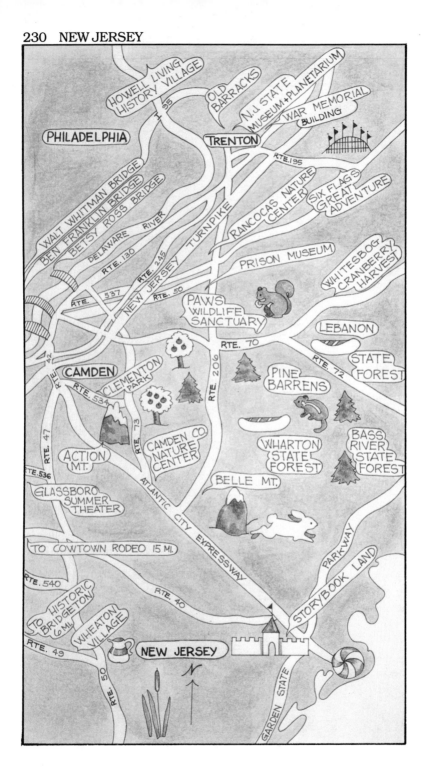

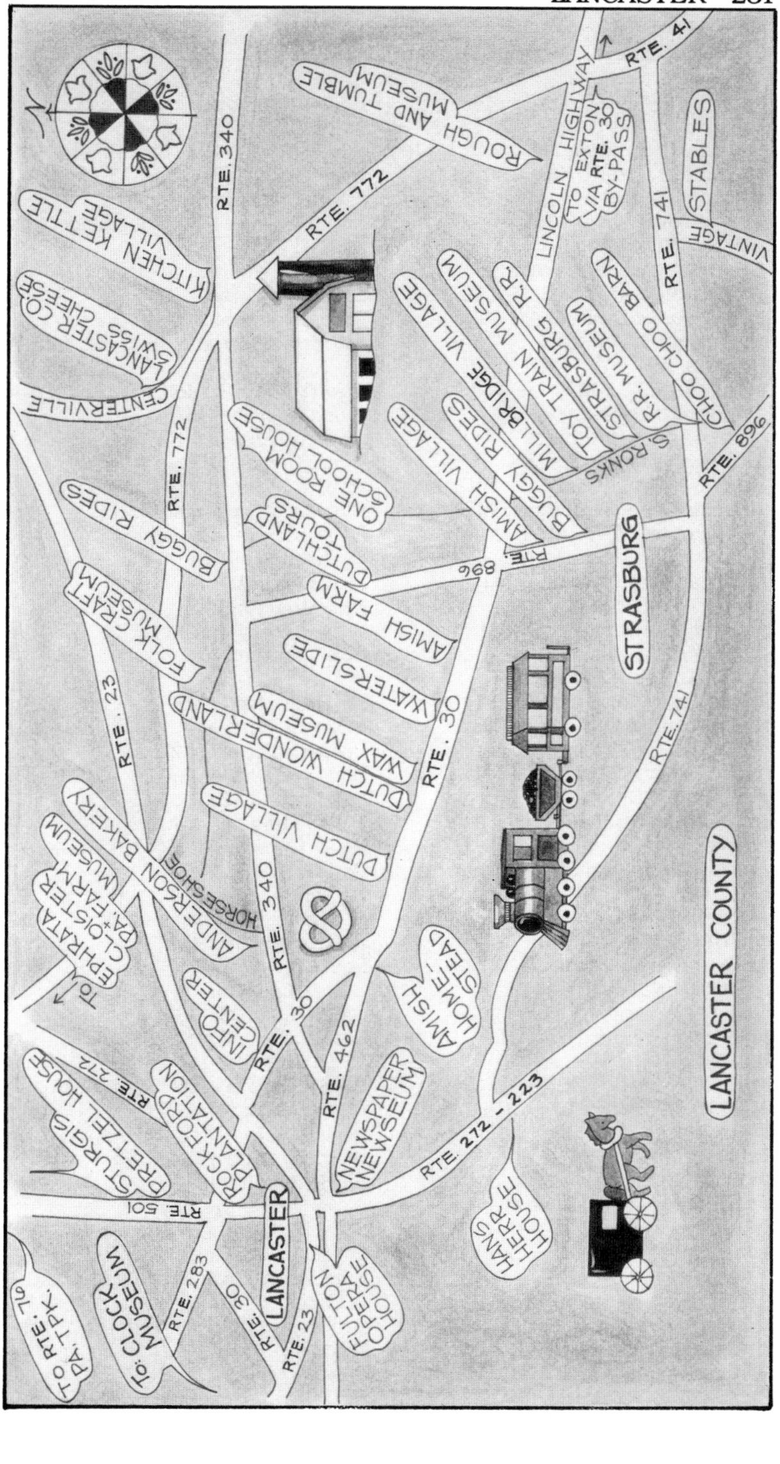
LANCASTER COUNTY
LANCASTER
STRASBURG
ROUGH AND TUMBLE MUSEUM
KITCHEN KETTLE VILLAGE
LANCASTER CO. SWISS CHEESE
CENTERVILLE
ONE ROOM SCHOOL HOUSE
DUTCHLAND TOURS
BUGGY RIDES
FOLK CRAFT MUSEUM
AMISH FARM
WATERSLIDE
WAX MUSEUM
DUTCH WONDERLAND
DUTCH VILLAGE
ANDERSON BAKERY
HORSESHOE
TO: EPHRATA CLOISTER PA. FARM MUSEUM
INFO CENTER
AMISH HOMESTEAD
NEWSPAPER NEWSEUM
ROCKFORD PLANTATION
STURGIS PRETZEL HOUSE
TO: CLOCK MUSEUM
TO RTE. 716 PA. TPK.
FULTON OPERA HOUSE
HANS HERR HOUSE
AMISH VILLAGE
BUGGY RIDES
MILL BRIDGE VILLAGE
TOY TRAIN MUSEUM
STRASBURG R.R.
STRASBURG R.R. MUSEUM
CHOO CHOO BARN
S. RONKS
VINTAGE
STABLES
LINCOLN HIGHWAY
TO EXTON VIA RTE. 30 BY-PASS
RTE. 41
RTE. 340
RTE. 772
RTE. 23
RTE. 30
RTE. 462
RTE. 272
RTE. 501
RTE. 283
RTE. 272 - 223
RTE. 896
RTE. 741